I0333781

Tafsir
Sūrat al-Fātiḥa

Sayyid Sadek Al-Moussawi

First Edition Published in 2023
AHLULBAYT ISLAMIC MISSION (AIM)
aimislam.com

ISBN: 978-0-9957589-5-7

SŪRAT AL-FĀTIḤA
(The Opening)

بِسۡمِ ٱللَّهِ ٱلرَّحۡمَٰنِ ٱلرَّحِيمِ ١

ٱلۡحَمۡدُ لِلَّهِ رَبِّ ٱلۡعَٰلَمِينَ ٢ ٱلرَّحۡمَٰنِ ٱلرَّحِيمِ ٣

مَٰلِكِ يَوۡمِ ٱلدِّينِ ٤ إِيَّاكَ نَعۡبُدُ وَإِيَّاكَ نَسۡتَعِينُ

٥ ٱهۡدِنَا ٱلصِّرَٰطَ ٱلۡمُسۡتَقِيمَ ٦ صِرَٰطَ ٱلَّذِينَ أَنۡعَمۡتَ

عَلَيۡهِمۡ غَيۡرِ ٱلۡمَغۡضُوبِ عَلَيۡهِمۡ وَلَا ٱلضَّآلِّينَ ٧

In the Name of God, the Compassionate, the Merciful.

Praise be to God, Lord of the Worlds,

The Compassionate, the Merciful.

Master of the Day of Judgment,

You [alone] do we worship, and You [alone] do we ask for aid,

Guide us to the Straight Path,

The path of those upon whom You have bestowed favour, not of those who have evoked Your wrath or of those who are astray.

[Holy Qur'an : Chapter 1]

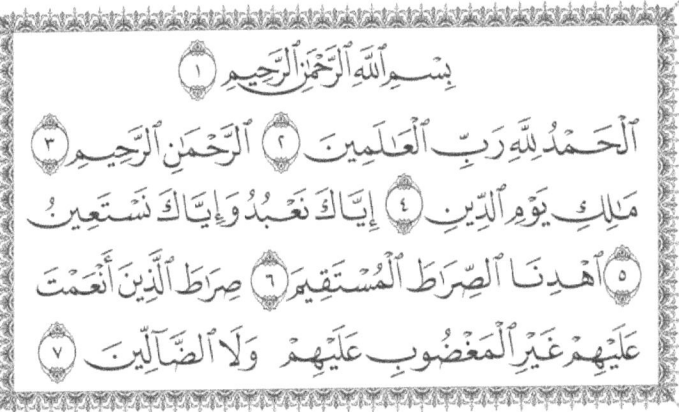

Peace be upon our mother, Fāṭima al-Zahrā (as),
To her I dedicate these words which God has blessed me with writing.

TABLE OF CONTENTS

Introduction 11

Prayer: The Pillar of Religion 13

Sūrat al-Fātiḥa: An Essential Component of Prayer 15

Sūrat al-Fātiḥa: General Overview 16

Virtues of Sūrat al-Fātiḥa 19

Chapter One: The Basmala 23

Allāh: The One and Only 27

Grammatical Structure of the Basmala 30

Two Attributes of Mercy: Raḥmān and Raḥīm 31

Inclusiveness of Divine Mercy Denoted by Ar-Raḥmān 32

Specificity of Divine Mercy Denoted by Ar-Raḥīm 33

Manifestations of Specific Divine Mercy 34

Divine Names and the Human Purification of the Self 43

Mercy to Mankind: Prophet Muḥammad (s) 45

Chapter Two: Boundless Praise 51

Grammatical Structure 55

Why is the word Rabb (Lord) used and not another Divine Name? 56

What does the term ʿālamīn denote? 58

Gratitude to God for Guidance to Faith 60
Gratitude to God for the Conferment of Favors 63
A Grateful Heart 66
When should we offer praise to God? 67
How should we offer praise? 69

Chapter Three: Overflowing Mercy 73
Reflections on this Quranic verse: 76
The Most-Merciful of the Merciful 77

Chapter Four: Majestic Sovereignty 81
Reflections on the verse: 85
Recitation Variants 87
Why is sovereignty over Judgement Day specifically mentioned in Sūrat al-Fātiḥa? 89
Names of Judgement Day 90

Chapter Five: Humble Devotion 93
Reflections on the Holy Verse: 97
Difference between Isti'āna and Isti'ātha 100
The Purpose of Existence 102
Continuous Worship 104
Transformation of Ordinary Actions into Acts of Worship 105
How sincere are we when we recite "You [alone] do we worship"? 107

Results of Seeking Divine Assistance 109
Divine Assistance 111

Chapter Six: Divine Guidance 113
Reflections on the Holy Verse:.. 119
Divine Guidance 120
Requirements of Guidance.. 125
Specification of the Straight Path.................................. 132
Contributors to Guidance... 142
Guidance to the Straight Path... 151

Chapter Seven: Heavenly Favor 155
Reflections on the Holy Verse:.. 158
The People of Favor 161
Forms of Spiritual Favors... 163
Those Who Have Evoked God's Wrath........................ 168
Those Who Are astray 171

Postscript 175
A Lesson from an Afflicted Man 177
A Bedouin on the Verge of Death 178
A Lesson from an Impoverished Man........................... 178

Introduction

"Even this prayer is Thy gift and lesson (to us);
else, wherefore has a rose-bed grown in an ash-pit?"[1]

-Rumi

PRAYER: THE PILLAR OF RELIGION

Have you reflected over your prayers? Do you intend to turn your prayer into an elevated spiritual experience? If so, this book is for you.

As Muslims, we turn to God five times per day; whether at home in our familiar surroundings or on a long journey filled with new experiences, during favorable weather conditions or in harsh temperatures, when we enjoy good health or suffer sickness, in times of security or fear, during periods of ease or turmoil –our lives are always marked by a return to God.

The importance that we Muslims attach to prayer and our unfaltering adherence to it has inspired non-Muslims with awe. "Even in its external forms alone, the Islamic mode of worship has held a profound fascination

1. Nicholson, Reynold Alleyne. The Mathnawí of Jalálu'ddín Rúmí. Brill: 1972, p.231 (Electronic Format).

for outside observers down through the ages. Many an imagination has been captured by the haunting sound of the Call to Prayer: 'Allāhu Akbar! Allāhu Akbar!' or by the stunning spectacle of row upon row of worshippers bowing and prostrating themselves in perfect unison during Friday Congregation in the concourse of some splendid yet at the same time starkly simple mosque."[1]

The earnest and vibrant Muslim performance of prayer caught the attention of Riccold de Monte Croce, a Dominican missionary from Florence who set out for the Middle East in 1288. He was inspired to the extent that he wrote: "What shall I say of their prayer? For they pray with such concentration and devotion that I was astonished when I was able to see it personally and observe it with my own eyes."[2]

Prayer is our defining aspect as Muslims; the pillar of religion, the deed most beloved to God when offered on time, and the key to paradise[3]. It is the most superior form of munājāt, an "intimate conversation" with God, and a form of communication with the Creator. It establishes a spiritual bond that links humans with God, allowing them to offer praise and make sincere entreaties to their Lord.

1. Holland, Muhtar. Translator's Foreword. Inner Dimensions of Islamic Worship (translated from the Iḥyā') by Al-Ghazālī. The Islamic Foundation: 1983, p.23. Italics not part of the original text.
2. Katz, Marion Holmes. Prayer in Islamic Thought and Practice. Cambridge University Press: 2013, p.2.
3. These descriptions of prayer are mentioned in ḥadīths transmitted from Prophet Muḥammad (as).

SŪRAT AL-FĀTIḤA: AN ESSENTIAL COMPONENT OF PRAYER

Taking the sublime status of prayer into consideration, it is clear that we should grant special attention to each component of prayer in order to attain spiritual elevation. Awareness of the various dimensions of prayer enables a person to offer worship with a heightened sense of spirituality. When this is achieved, prayer is transformed from a duty which some individuals might perform mechanically and with a wandering mind into a life-altering and rewarding experience. Expounding on prayer requires comprehensive volumes that provide explanation of all of its various components, but this book will embark on presenting an in-depth interpretation of one essential component of prayer: Sūrat al-Fātiḥa.

Recitation of sūrat al-Fātiḥa, the opening sūra of the Quran, is required in every prayer. A ḥadīth transmitted from Prophet Muḥammad (s) states that: "There is no prayer for one who does not recite Fātiḥat al-Kitāb (The Opening of the Book)."[1] Hence, the obligation to recite Sūrat al-Fātiḥa in each prayer entails concentration on the meanings of this sūra. Additionally, Muslim males and females are urged to seek knowledge. The foremost priority is to attain knowledge of the Quran, God's Holy Word. Not only can knowledge of the meanings of the verses of Sūrat al-Fātiḥa enhance spirituality in prayer, but this knowledge can also be a step in our personal

1. This ḥadīth is mentioned with slightly different wordings in books of ḥadīth compilations.

Refer to: Al-Nūrī, Mustadrak al-Wasā'el. Mu'asasat Āl al-Bayt li Iḥyā' al-Turāth: 1988. Volume 4, p.158.

endeavor to formulate an in-depth knowledge of Quranic sūras and form an active bond with the Book of God.

SŪRAT AL-FĀTIḤA: GENERAL OVERVIEW

Have you ever wondered why Sūrat al-Fātiḥa has been specifically chosen by God to be recited in each prayer? With 114 sūras in the Quran, what eminent status does Sūrat al-Fātiḥa hold?

Sūrat al-Fātiḥa contains fundamental Quranic doctrinal principles, and hence a deep study of this sūra forms a basis for general Quranic knowledge. Sūrat al-Fātiḥa serves as a defining feature of Muslim identity, inspiring believers with a sense of responsibility and action. Hence, the significance of this highly-venerated sūra can never be overemphasized. In what follows is a brief overview of Sūrat al-Fātiḥa before we embark on a detailed verse by verse interpretation.

Sūrat al-Fātiḥa is the first chapter of the Quran, and is considered by the vast majority of scholars to be among the first sūras to have been revealed in Mecca. The primary meaning of al-Fātiḥa is "the Opening," which indicates the sūra's function as "the opening of the Book" (Fātiḥat al-Kitāb)[1]. A ḥadīth transmitted from Prophet Muḥammad (s) mentions that the greatest sūra revealed in the Quran is Sūrat al-Fātiḥa[2]. The elevated status of this sūra arises from its content which summarizes one of the foremost aims of the Quran: to establish a firm monotheistic belief

1. The Study Quran, p.64.
2. Mogra, Imran. Understanding Islam: A Guide for Teachers. SAGE Publishing: 2020.

in the reader and urge virtuous conduct. Hence, recitation of Sūrat al-Fātiḥa, with adherence to its content fulfills a spiritual-practical purpose.

Muslims regard Sūrat al-Fātiḥa with high reverence and recite it in a wide variety of contexts such as during weddings, as a remedy for sickness, before setting out on an important trip, and in funeral ceremonies. "As it is the first sūra in the Quran and the centerpiece of Muslim daily prayer, this concise passage plays a much wider role in Muslim life. It is the first part of the Quran that children learn – and it opens their education. In schools they can be heard chanting it in groups. Learning it in Arabic gives it a unifying function between Muslims throughout the world, it inspires non-Arabs to start learning more Arabic later in life. Its blessing is sought on numerous occasions in Muslims' lives."[1]

The importance of Sūrat al-Fātiḥa is emphasized in a Quranic verse where it is given a special appellation that takes into account the sūra's composition of seven verses:

> "And We have given you, [O Muḥammad], Sab' al-Mathānī (The Seven Oft-Repeated [verses]) and the Great Quran" (Quran 15:87)

This verse mentions Sūrat al-Fātiḥa independently alongside the Quran, thus emphasizing its status. Even though Sūrat al-Fātiḥa is part of the Quran, but mentioning it alongside the Quran serves to highlight its importance.

---

1. Abdel Haleem, Muḥammad. Understanding the Qur'an: Themes and Style. I.B. Tauris: 2011, p.27.

A swift contemplation of Sūrat al-Fātiḥa shows how this sūra encompasses several major doctrinal principles which are present in implicit or clear references to:

- Monotheism ("The Compassionate, The Merciful");
- Prophecy ("The path of those upon whom You have bestowed favor"); and,
- Resurrection ("Master of the Day of Judgment").

Sūrat al-Fātiḥa also fulfills a spiritual-emotional purpose:

- It vibrates with devotion to God who is the source of all favors ("Praise be to God");
- Invokes a sense of divine providence ("Lord of the Worlds");
- Lays stress on worship ("You [alone] do We worship);
- Reminds humans that assistance is solely granted by God (And You [alone] do we ask for aid").

The tone of Sūrat al-Fātiḥa differs from other Quranic sūras in that it serves an instructive purpose. Through this sūra, God teaches humans how to address Him and what favors to ask of Him. The following ḥadīth transmitted from Prophet Muḥammad (s) shows how Sūrat al-Fātiḥa to be "a remarkable experience of worship indeed, involving believers and God throughout. The believer recites each of the short verses, knowing that God responds to every statement s/he makes"[1]:

> "God (Mighty and Sublime) said: 'I have divided prayer between Myself and My servant into two

1. Understanding the Qur'an, p.21-22.

halves, and My servant shall have what he has asked for.'

When the servant says, 'Praise be to God, Lord of the Worlds,' God (Mighty and Sublime) says, 'My servant has praised Me.'

And when he says, 'The Compassionate, the Merciful,' God (Mighty and Sublime) says, 'My servant has extolled Me.'

And when he says, 'Master of the Day of Judgment,' God (Mighty and Sublime) says, 'My servant has glorified Me.'

And when he says, 'You [alone] do We worship, and You [alone] do we ask for aid,' [God] says, 'This is between Me and My servant, and My servant shall have what he has asked for.'

And when he says, 'Guide us [to] the Straight Path. The path of those upon whom You have bestowed favor, not of those who have evoked [Your] wrath or of those who are astray,' [God] says, 'This is for My servant, and My servant shall have what he has asked for.'"[1]

VIRTUES OF SŪRAT AL-FĀTIḤA

Reward for Recitation

It is transmitted that the Prophet Muḥammad (s) said: "A Muslim who recites Fātiḥat al-Kitāb (the Opening of the Book) will be granted the reward [of] reciting two-thirds

1. Ḥadīth translated with reference to the previous source, p.22.

of the Quran, and will be granted the reward [of] giving charity to every believing male and believing female."[1]

This high reward may be explained by taking the content of Sūrat al-Fātiḥa into account. The Quran in general consists of three main principles: Calling people to God, informing them of Resurrection Day, and teaching them divine laws so that they may adhere to these laws in the individual and social sphere. Sūrat al-Fātiḥa contains a reference to the first two mentioned principles, and in view of this we might understand why recitation of this sūra entails two-thirds of the reward granted for reciting the entire Quran.

Cure for Sickness

There are means to sustenance, health and wealth, and all of these means lie exclusively in the hands of God. Many humans restrict their vision to a materialistic worldview and pay no heed to the divine origin of this universe or God's direction of the affairs of mankind. Believers, on the other hand, know that God manages their lives, and that whatever grace they enjoy is a blessing from God whether this divine favor comes in the image of a loving spouse, a healthy child, security, financial stability or recovery from sickness and pain, to mention but a few.

Sūrat al-Fātiḥa has special significance in Islamic ḥadīths. Prophet Muḥammad (s) is reported as saying to his companion, Jāber al-Ansārī: "It (Sūrat al-Fātiḥa) is a cure for every ailment except death."[2]

1. Al-Shīrāzī, Nāṣer Makārem. Al-Amthal fī Tafsīr Kitāb Allāh al-Munazzal. Dar al-Amīra: 2005. Volume 1, p.16.
2. Rayshahrī, Moḥammad. Mīzān al-Ḥikma. Volume 2, p.940.

Another narration states that: "If al-Ḥamd (Sūrat al-Fātiḥa) were recited over a dead person seventy times and his spirit were returned inside him, that would not be surprising."[1] This ḥadīth indicates the miraculous aspect of Sūrat al-Fātiḥa. This is not a cause for wonder. Prophets have been accompanied by miracles throughout history; Abraham was not burned by a raging fire, Moses' staff turned into a snake, and Jesus restored the dead to life. The Quran is an enduring miracle, and thus both worldly and other-worldly rewards are granted to the reader of the Quran who has a pure heart and a firm conviction. From this introduction, we may turn to a profound study of Sūrat al-Fātiḥa taking into account the various aspects of this holy text.

This publication is part of a successive chain of efforts undergone by Muslim scholars and commentators throughout history and until our modern times to provide insight into Sūrat al-Fātiḥa. This care and diligence arises from the elevated status of this sūra which contains the essence of the Quran. More contributions will follow, God-willing.

And now with a recitation of Sūrat al-Fātiḥa, we open this book.

1. Al-Kulaynī, Moḥammad bin al-Ḥasan. Al-Kāfī: 2000. Volume 2, p.623.

بِسْمِ ٱللَّهِ ٱلرَّحْمَٰنِ ٱلرَّحِيمِ ﴿١﴾

1. In the name of Allah, the Entirely Merciful, the Especially Merciful.

ٱلْحَمْدُ لِلَّهِ رَبِّ ٱلْعَالَمِينَ ﴿٢﴾

2. [All] praise is [due] to Allah, Lord of the worlds –

ٱلرَّحْمَٰنِ ٱلرَّحِيمِ ﴿٣﴾

3. The Entirely Merciful, the Especially Merciful,

مَالِكِ يَوْمِ ٱلدِّينِ ﴿٤﴾

4. Sovereign of the Day of Recompense

إِيَّاكَ نَعْبُدُ وَإِيَّاكَ نَسْتَعِينُ ﴿٥﴾

5. It is You we worship and You we ask for help.

ٱهْدِنَا ٱلصِّرَاطَ ٱلْمُسْتَقِيمَ ﴿٦﴾

6. Guide us to the straight path –

صِرَاطَ الَّذِينَ أَنعَمتَ عَلَيهِمْ غَيرِ المغضُوبِ عَلَيهِمْ وَلاَ الضَّالِّينَ ﴿٧﴾

7. The path of those upon whom You have bestowed favor, not of those who have earned [Your] anger or of those who are astray.

Chapter One:

The Basmala

بِسْمِ ٱللَّهِ ٱلرَّحْمَٰنِ ٱلرَّحِيمِ ﴿١﴾

1. In the Name of God, the Compassionate, the Merciful

THE BASMALA, which corresponds to the phrase "In the Name of God, the Compassionate, the Merciful" is included before each sūra of the Quran, except for the ninth sūra. The two divine attributes ar-Raḥmān and ar-Raḥīm, which have been translated here into "the Compassionate, the Merciful", have no precise English equivalents. Translations strive to come close to the original meanings as far as possible, but the English formula of the basmala may differ from one translated text to another since there are no precise equivalents in English.

Muslims hold the basmala in special reverence and recite it in a wide variety of contexts: before performing an important action, prior to eating and drinking, or when in fear of a certain danger. Invoking the name of God before significant events imparts a sense of consecration on human action. The importance of the basmala is emphasized when we take into account that the first revealed verse of the Quran, delivered by the angel

Gabriel (as) to Prophet Muḥammad (s), urges the Prophet (s) to invoke the name of God:

> "Read in the Name of your Lord who created." (Quran 96:1)

The basmala serves as a defining formula in Islam. Even non-Muslims dwell on the depth of this concise, but meaning-rich verse: "...right from the first verses of the first chapter we begin to learn much about God's compassion and mercy. We are confronted with it, surprised by it, drawn into it. This is a core truth of Islam, repeated over and over, and neither the bigoted nor the violent can obscure the fact."[1]

Recitation of the basmala before performing actions signifies dependence on God's power alone and not on personal abilities. It also suggests an intention to draw close to God, and thus transforms normal actions into a form of worship. In this manner, consuming food, driving your car, or going to work gains a spiritual meaning. A ḥadīth transmitted from Imam 'Alī (as) states: "If a servant [of God] intends to recite or perform an action and says 'In the Name of God, the Compassionate, the Merciful", [his action] is blessed."[2] Another ḥadīth transmitted from Imam Muḥammad al-Bāqer (as) mentions that one should recite the basmala before commencing any action,

---

1. Clooney, Francis. "Discovering God's Mercy in the Quran". America Magazine. December 11, 2015.
2. Al-Majlisī. Biḥār al-Anwār. Dār Iḥyā' al-Turāth al-'Arabī: 1983. Volume 92, p.242.

whether this action is important or trivial, so that it will be blessed.[1]

Invoking God's name stretches back among believers to ancient times and reflects a firm belief in divine providence. The Quran recounts the story of the Great Flood and presents a vivid image of Noah's speech to the ark's passengers and invoking God's name before the ark's journey over mountain-sized, perilous waves:

> "And he said: 'Embark on it, in the name of God be its sailing and its anchoring; most surely my Lord is Forgiving, Merciful.'" (Quran 11:41)

This usage is further reflected in the letter King Solomon sent to the Queen of Sheba urging her and her people to convert to monotheism and forsake sun-worship. The letter included a phrase which captured the queen's attention and drove her to remark to the nobles around her:

> "Indeed, it is from Solomon, and indeed, it [reads]: 'In the name of God, the Compassionate, the Merciful.'" (Quran 27:30)

ALLĀH: THE ONE AND ONLY

In the Arabic language, Allāh refers to God. "Allāh" occurs well over 2,500 times in the Quran[2], and it encompasses all of the Divine Attributes: "Allāh is not only the most

1. Ibid. Volume 16, p.461.
2. Rahman, Fazlur. Major Themes of the Qur'an. The University of Chicago Press: 2009, p.1.

universal and all-embracing Name, but also the most specific of the Divine Names in that it cannot be used to describe any being other than God."[1]

The following valuable explanations until the next heading are all derived from the book Key to al-Fatiha: Understanding the Basic Concepts: The Arabic root of the word Allāh is ALH. Words that derive from this Arabic root have the following meanings which illustrate some of the attributes of Allāh:

A- **To be bewildered or perplexed.** No one is able to perceive and comprehend the exact nature and personality of Allāh. The human mind has always remained astonished and bewildered about Him.

"There is nothing like unto Him, and He is the Hearing, the Seeing." (Quran 42:11)

B- **To get satisfaction or to find comfort from someone's company or by seeking his protection.** It is only when a person establishes a true relationship with Allāh that he attains satisfaction and contentment.

"Those who have believed and whose hearts are assured by the remembrance of Allāh. Verily, in the remembrance of Allāh are hearts assured." (Quran 13:28)

C- **To have intense attachment and love for somebody or something.** All creatures love their creator. Allāh being the Supreme Creator infuses the feeling of affection and love among His creation.

1. The Study Quran, p.69.

"But those who believe are stronger in love for Allāh." (Quran 2:165)

D- **To be hidden or to remain concealed.** It is obvious that Allāh cannot be seen or perceived by anyone.

"Vision perceives Him not, but He perceives [all] vision; and He is the Subtle, the Aware." (Quran 6:103)

Although we cannot perceive Allāh, He is very close to us.

"And We are nearer to him than (his) jugular vein." (Quran 50:16)

E- **To worship someone.** The one who deserves to be worshipped should be the One who can fulfill the needs of the worshipper and give him satisfaction. It is only Allāh who provides all the necessary provisions for all his creatures to survive and He is the One who fulfills their needs and gives them satisfaction. Thus, He is the one who should be worshipped.

All these meanings have a logical relationship with each other. The concept of Allāh evokes intense love and awe that compels the entire universe to bow down before Him in submission. As He is the sole Creator He should be worshipped exclusively and obeyed without reservation. His remembrance is the source of satisfaction and comfort. He is the sole Sovereign. The Mightiest, the Greatest, and His Rule should override all human affairs.

The word Allāh is unique and almost incapable of translation into any other language. The English word

"God" with a capital "G" does not convey the array of meanings outlined above. Allāh is the personal name of the Ultimate Reality in this universe.[1]

GRAMMATICAL STRUCTURE OF THE BASMALA

A preceding verb is implied but not mentioned before the basmala. Thus, the meaning may be "I **commence** in the Name of God" or "I **seek aid** in the Name of God". This emphasizes that even everyday actions which are considered ordinary and worldly may take on a spiritual meaning.

When the presence of God is sensed, every hardship is eased and every pain is alleviated. Allāh's name eliminates inner turmoil and places tranquility in the heart. An account transmitted from Jāber bin 'Abd-Allāh relates how Jāber once accompanied Prophet Muḥammad (s) during one of his travels in the summer. On their way back, they reached a valley abounding with trees and they dispersed beneath their shade. While Prophet Muḥammad (s) was sleeping under a tree, a Bedouin crept near and raised his sword to deal him a blow. Prophet Muḥammad (s) awoke before the blade could descend upon him, and the Bedouin asked him: "O Muḥammad, who will guard you from me?"

Prophet Muḥammad (s) answered: "Allāh."

The Bedouin repeated his question a second then a third time: "Who will guard you from me?" but Prophet

1. Siddiqui, Abdur Rashid. Key to al-Fatiha: Understanding the Basic Concepts. The Islamic Foundation, 2001. P.2-4.

Muḥammad (s) unflinchingly provided the same answer: "Allāh."

This caused the bedouin to become agitated and he faltered. His hand trembled and his sword fell to the ground, but Prophet Muḥammad (s) lifted the sword and forgave the man his transgression. This report serves to demonstrate how mention of God's name soothes the heart, inspires one with fortitude, and links all actions to God regardless of the outcome.

TWO ATTRIBUTES OF MERCY: RAḤMĀN AND RAḤĪM

Mercy (ar-Raḥmā) is mentioned in two forms in the basmala to represent attributes of God: ar-Raḥmān and ar-Raḥīm. The former refers to the greatness and all-inclusiveness of divine mercy, while the latter refers to its endurance and stability.[1] As mentioned previously, various English translations have been given to the two divine attributes ar-Raḥmān and ar-Raḥīm, but the equivalents fail to provide the essence of the meanings in Arabic. "In the conventional translation of the basmala quoted above, the interpretation of the two names ar-Raḥmān and ar-Raḥīm as 'the Compassionate' and 'the Merciful' is only approximate as there is no real equivalent."[2]

1. Al-Amthal. Volume 1, p.26.
2. Introduction to Sufi Doctrine, p.36.

INCLUSIVENESS OF DIVINE MERCY DENOTED BY AR-RAḤMĀN

It is important to point out that Ar-Raḥmān is a title of an independent Quranic surah. Ar-Raḥmān is a Divine Name which denotes the magnitude of God's mercy that encompasses all humans, regardless if they are believers or non-believers, virtuous individuals or sinners. This is indicated in the holy verse:

> "Say: As for him who is in error, the Compassionate (ar-Raḥmān) will extend for him an extension until, when they behold that which they were promised, either torment or the Hour, they will know who is worst in position and who is weaker as an army." (Quran 19:75)

Some manifestations of inclusive mercy, denoted by the attribute ar-Raḥmān, pertain to aspects of creation such as our presence on a planet conducive to life, and the existence of natural phenomena like rain, sunlight, and the motion of night and day. This general mercy also pertains to divine endowments upon humans such as mental capacities, physical prowess, vital instincts, and the religious inclination (fitra) which drives mankind toward God. These grants are provided to all humans regardless of race or geographical region.

The encompassing mercy of God is referred to in a supplication which is recited in the month of Rajab: "O He who bestows upon one who asks Him, O He who bestows upon one who does not ask Him and does not know Him, out of His compassion and mercy."

The Quran mentions two factions: those who desire the worldly life and those who aim for the hereafter. The fate of each group differs in eternity; the former will find punishment while the latter will earn eternal bliss. Nonetheless, the Quran mentions that both factions receive divine bounty in this world:

> "Each do We supply, both these and those, from the bounty of your Lord. And the bounty of your Lord is not confined." (Quran 17:20)

In this manner, and "according to the majority of the exegetes, Raḥmān has the sense of Allāh who exercises His mercy and His compassion towards the entirety of His creation by providing that creation with that which it needs for its material and non-material existence. In other words, the manifestation of Raḥmān reaches every particle of created being, all orders of being; it reaches the mineral realm, the vegetable realm, the animal realm, and the human realm. And within the human realm it makes no distinction between the believer and the non-believer, between the virtuous and the sinner; everyone and all things benefit from the attribute of Raḥmān."[1]

SPECIFICITY OF DIVINE MERCY DENOTED BY AR-RAḤĪM

Ar-Raḥīm, however, refers to a special kind of mercy which is granted to the faithful. This is indicated in the holy verse:

1. Saaleh, Abdurrahman. Review: Surat Al-Fatiha: Foundation of the Qur'an by Hamid Algar. Islamic Studies, vol.43, no.4, 2004, p.684.

> "It is He who blesses you, and His angels, that He may bring you out from darkness into the light. And He is Merciful (Raḥīm) to the believers." (Quran 33:43)

> "He is unto them Gentle [and] Merciful (Raḥīm)." (Quran 9:117)

A ḥadīth transmitted from Prophet Muḥammad (s) states that God has 100 mercies. He lowered one to the Earth and distributed it upon His creatures, and through this single mercy, creatures show compassion to one another. He kept ninety-nine mercies for Judgment Day to show mercy to His servants. In what follows is a short explanation of some forms of divine mercy which are solely granted to the believers.

MANIFESTATIONS OF SPECIFIC DIVINE MERCY

Tranquility in Times of Tribulation

Believers enjoy the special mercy of God -denoted by the attribute ar-Raḥīm- in various instances. One manifestation of this mercy is the tranquility which God bestows upon believers during periods of hardship:

> "Those who have believed and whose hearts are assured by the remembrance of Allāh. Verily, in the remembrance of Allāh are hearts assured." (Quran 13:28)

To gain more insight into this special mercy, consider the following incident which occurred in the early period of Islam. The persecution of the pagan Quraysh increased against Prophet Muḥammad (s), and this compelled the Prophet (s) to make the decision to leave his hometown of Mecca and escape oppression. On the night of his departure, the Prophet's house was besieged by men from Quraysh who meant to assassinate him, but he was able to flee without attracting their notice. The assassins raided his home only to find Imam 'Alī (as) in his bed.

The Meccans were not deterred and sent men to follow the Prophet (s) and seize him. Prophet Muḥammad (s) and his companion found refuge in a cave near the summit of the mountain of Thawr overlooking Mecca. The pursuers followed their tracks and reached the mouth of the cave they were hiding in but did not enter as they saw signs which indicated that none had entered the cave. In these moments of imminent danger, Prophet Muḥammad (s) in his unshakable faith found serenity. The Quran refers to this incident in the holy verse:

> "If you do not aid him [the Prophet]- God has already aided him when those who disbelieved had driven him out [of Mecca] as one of two, when they were in the cave, when he said to his companion, 'Do not grieve; verily, God is with us.' Then God sent down his tranquility upon him and supported him with forces you did not see and made the word of those who disbelieved the lowest, while the word of God is the highest. And God is Mighty [and] Wise." (Quran 9:40)

Another historical instance briefly referred to in the Quran demonstrates the special mercy granted to the believers. The following account is derived from the book

A Restatement of the History of Islam & Muslims C.E. 570 to 661. After the conquest of Mecca, Muslims increased in number and military might. Prophet Muḥammad (s) received intelligence that the enemy tribes of Thaqeef and Hawazin had left their home base and were approaching Mecca. When these reports were confirmed, Prophet Muḥammad (s) ordered a general mobilization in the newly-conquered city. The Prophet did not want Mecca to become a battle-ground, so he left the city at the head of 12,000 warriors to meet the enemy. But when the first column constituting the Muslim vanguard entered the valley of Ḥunayn in the south-east of Mecca, the enemy was already lying-in ambush.

The pass was narrow, the road was very rough, and the Muslims were advancing unaware of the enemy's presence. It was just before dawn when all of a sudden, the Hawazin launched their attack. The surprise was complete and the charge of the enemy was so impetuous that the Muslims could not withstand it. The Muslim vanguard broke and fled, and the main body of the army was just behind. The first column ran into its face and struck panic into its men so that they also turned their backs to the enemy and began to flee. It was not long before Prophet Muḥammad (s) was left alone with only a few of his faithful followers around him who firmly stood their ground.

The Prophet (s) asked his uncle, 'Abbās, to call the fleeing Muslims. 'Abbās had a very powerful voice, and his voice boomed in the narrow valley and almost everyone heard it. This proved effective in checking the flight of the Muslims. The Ansār were the first to halt and return to battle. Inspired by their example, others also rallied and soon the Muslim army was able to regroup. A fierce skirmish took place. At first, the issue appeared uncertain but then the Muslims began to press the enemy. Once they recovered their morale, they went on the offensive and pressed their advantage, and then it was the enemy who was running in all directions.[1]

A reference to this battle and the tranquility God granted the believers is mentioned in the Quran:

> "God has given you victory in many battlefields and on the day of Ḥunayn when your great numbers pleased you, but they availed you naught. The land, for all that it is wide, did constrain you, and you turned back in retreat.
> Then God sent down His tranquility upon His Messenger and upon the believers, and sent down forces which you saw not, and punished the disbelievers; and that is the reward of the disbelievers." (Quran 25-26)

A third account takes us back earlier in history, to the exodus of the Israelites from Egypt under the leadership of Moses. After facing oppression at the hands of Pharaoh, God ordered Moses to lead the Israelites in their flight from Egypt by night. When Pharaoh learned of their escape, he speedily gathered an army and went in pursuit, overtaking the Israelites by the sea. The fugitives were overtaken with fear and felt helpless as they now faced an impasse: the sea was in front of them and a hostile army was gathered behind them. Nevertheless, in these moments of distress, Moses was certain that God would

1. Razwy, Ali Asghar. A Restatement of the History of Islam & Muslims C.E. 570 to 661.

not forsake him. God ordered Moses to strike the sea with his staff, and it was split into two allowing the Israelites to pass to safety.[1]

The Holy Quran mentions the fear of the Israelites at being overtaken and at the same time shows us the firm conviction of Moses:

> "And when the two companies saw one another, the companions of Moses said, 'Indeed, we are to be overtaken!'
> [Moses] said: No! surely my Lord is with me; He will guide me.'" (Quran 26:61-62)

Divine Answers to Prayer

The divine response to supplication is another manifestation of the mercy which is granted to the believers. The Quran relates how various prophets were granted relief and divine bounty after periods of suffering.

---

1. The abandonment of faith, however, leads to adverse results and the inevitable loss of the special mercy which is granted to the believers. After the Israelites fled from Pharaoh, they came upon a group of people who were worshiping idols. When Moses answered God's call and spent forty nights away from his people, the Israelites began to worship a golden calf constructed in Moses's absence instead of worshipping the One, Unseen God who had delivered them from Pharaoh and split the sea so they could pass to safety. Moses was appalled when he returned; he burnt the calf, shattered it to pieces, and scattered it in the water. After this incident, the Quran states the following supplication by Moses: "My Lord, forgive me and my brother and admit us into Your mercy, for You are the Most-Merciful of the merciful.'" (Quran 7:151)

- God rescued Noah from the Great Flood with his household:

  "And [mention] Noah, when he called [to God] aforetime, so We responded to him and saved him and his family from the great affliction." (Quran 21:76)

- God healed Job from his ailment and granted him the family he had lost:

  "And [mention] Job, when he cried to his Lord, 'Indeed, adversity has touched me, and you are the Most-Merciful of the merciful.'
  So, We answered him, and removed the affliction that was upon him, and We gave him his household [that he had lost] and the like thereof along with them, as a mercy from Us and a reminder for the worshippers [of God]." (Quran 21:83-84)

- God granted Zechariah a blessed son despite his advanced age and his wife's barrenness:

  "And [mention] Zechariah, when he called to his Lord, 'My Lord, do not leave me alone [with no heir], and you are the best of inheritors.'
  So, We responded to him, and granted him John, and amended for him his wife [to bear a child]. Indeed, they used to hasten to good deeds and supplicate Us in hope and fear, and they were to Us humble." (Quran 21:90)

- God rescued Jonah from the belly of the whale in response to his entreaties:

> "So, We responded to him and saved him from the distress, and thus do We save the believers." (Quran 21:88)

- And God saved Lot from the town which committed moral abominations:

  > "And unto Lot we gave judgment and knowledge, and We saved him from the town which committed abominations. Indeed, they were a people of evil, disobedient." (Quran 21:74)

It is important to state that it is not only prophets who receive God's bounty and blessings. Ordinary humans who are sincere and faithful to their Lord also gain divine favor and receive answers to their urgent prayers. God grants His servants relief after pain and suffering. He dries their tears and casts joy in their hearts after they had gone through so much anguish. Even in our everyday lives there are miracles to be noticed, if we only slow down to take account of these beautiful expressions of divine mercy.

Provision of Rizq

A third manifestation of divine mercy which is granted to the believers is rizq. Rizq is an Arabic word which may be translated into English as "provision" or "sustenance". This word, however, has a wider meaning and denotes all forms of divine bestowal. In view of this, every form of grace is included under the term rizq. Even though God distributes His bounty upon all humans whether they are believers or not, there is a form of rizq which is specifically granted to the faithful.

A ḥadīth transmitted from Imam 'Alī states: "Rizq is of two forms: one which you seek, and one which seeks you."[1] We may provide the following explanation: The first form of rizq requires personal effort. For instance, attainment of academic success, material wealth, or personal accomplishment entails an individual's exertion of mental and physical labor. On the other hand, the second form of rizq is a divine endowment that accompanies piety, as the following holy verse illustrates:

> "...And whoever fears God, [God] will make for him a way out [of difficulty],
> And will provide for him from where he does not expect. And whoever relies upon God, then He is sufficient for him. Indeed, God will accomplish His purpose. God has set a measure for all things." (Quran 65:2-3)

The faithful are aware of these two aspects of rizq; they pursue the familiar means but also know that they will gain special grace from God. Several ḥadīths indicate that acts of piety such as performing the recommended night vigil, paying charity, and upholding ties of kinship result in certain rewards in this worldly life even before the hereafter.

A ḥadīth transmitted from Imam Ja'far al-Ṣādiq (as) states that whoever is overly concerned with his rizq will be considered sinful. The ḥadīth goes on to mention how the Prophet Daniel lived in the time of an oppressive

1. Imam 'Alī. Nahj al-Balāghah. Dar al-Hijra, p.513.

tyrant who threw him inside a pit with predatory animals, but they did not approach him nor did they injure him. God entrusted another prophet to take food to Daniel, and when sustenance reached him, Daniel prayed: "Praise be to God who does not forget the one who mentions Him; praise be to God who rewards benevolence with benevolence, and patience with salvation." Imam Ja'far al-Ṣādiq (as) remarked at the close of this account that God gives the pious rizq from where they do not expect.[1]

In line with this, the Most-Merciful -ar-Raḥīm- encompasses his faithful servants with hidden graces; He bestows guidance upon them, and removes them out of darkness and admits them into the light. He saves them from perils, strengthens them during calamities, and grants them victory. The more a person exerts an effort to become closer to God, the higher the mercies s/he receives.

To further illustrate this point, consider the following Quranic account of the People of the Cave, a group of young men who lived in a pagan society but were persecuted for their belief in the One God and their repudiation of idol-worship:

> "And We strengthened their hearts when they stood up and said, 'Our Lord is the Lord of the heavens and the earth. Never will we invoke besides Him any deity. If we did, we would indeed have uttered an enormity!
> These our people have taken for worship gods other than Him: why do they not bring forward a clear authority regarding them? And who does more wrong than he who invents a falsehood against God?

1. Al-Āmilī, Al-Ḥor. Wasā'el al-Shī'a. Volume 17, p.56.

> And when you forsake them and what they worship other than God, then seek refuge in the cave. Your Lord will spread for you of His mercy, and will prepare for you from your affair facility." (Quran 18:14-16)

This story demonstrates how God's mercy encompasses His devoted and sincere servants. God ordained that they should sleep in their cave, and their miraculous slumber lasted for more than 300 years. They woke up in a different era, at a time when monotheism had prevailed in their community but doubt of resurrection had emerged. Their awakening came as a sign from God to re-establish belief in the bodily resurrection of the dead, and thus their awakening caused a doctrinal revival in society.

DIVINE NAMES AND THE HUMAN PURIFICATION OF THE SELF

The reference to God's Divine Names in the Quran not only serves to reveal the greatness of God. We may also conclude the necessity of adopting these divine attributes when they are accessible to humans. Every human who seeks perfectibility and closeness to God should assume the character traits of the Divine Names. God is Knowledgeable, so one should seek knowledge; God is Merciful, so one should display mercy to the creatures of God, and so forth. Individuals who more strongly represent these Divine Names attain more closeness to God.

When taking into consideration that every Quranic sūra (except one) opens with the basmala, and in view of the fact that God chose ar-Raḥmān and ar-Raḥīm from all of His Divine Names in the basmala, we may conclude that divine mercy is the essence of existence:

> "My mercy encompasses all things." (Quran 7:156)

In light of this, we should strive to adopt this quality of mercy and exhibit it in our daily lives: "The first step is to reflect on the ways in which compassion could improve your relations with others, not to mention your relations with yourself and the Eternal One. Then take stock of all the ways in which you already manifest compassion and identify areas for improvement. Think about specific ways to build compassion in your attitudes and actions, and then follow through with conscious thoughts or acts of compassion throughout the day. Renew your intention every morning, and keep track of your efforts through journaling or some kind of self-examination at the end of the day. Try to be conscious of every opportunity for a compassionate act or thought...Slowly but surely, 'little by little,' you will find that you are surrendering your judgmental, self-centered ego to the Compassionate One and you are ready to turn your attention to another divine attribute that you want to manifest in your life."[1]

MERCY TO MANKIND: PROPHET MUḤAMMAD (S)

The divine dispatch of prophets to guide their communities is a form of mercy. The Quran does not mention all

1. Rahman, Jamal; Schmitt Elias, Kathleen; Holmes Redding, Ann. Out of Darkness, Into Light. Morehouse Publishing: 2009, p.137.

prophets by name, but it maintains that a warner was sent to each nation:

> "And, indeed We have sent Messengers before you [O Muḥammad]; among them are those [whose stories] we have related to you, and among them are those [whose stories] We have not related to you." (Quran 40:78)

> "Verily, We have sent you with the truth, as a bearer of glad tidings and a warner. And there was no nation but there had passed within it a warner." (Quran 35:24)

Throughout the ages, God sent prophets to different nations, guiding people to the Truth, teaching them to maintain justice in their societies, and enjoining them to the performance of righteous deeds. The dispatch of Prophet Muḥammad (s) to mankind was a form of divine mercy, as God states in the Holy Quran.

> "And We have not sent you, [O Muḥammad], except as a mercy to the worlds." (Quran 21:107)

The call of Prophet Muḥammad (s) breathed life into the Arab society which had plunged into darkness and descended into immorality. In a moving speech which is still cited today, Jaʿfar bin Abī Ṭālib (as) eloquently expressed the principles of Islam which the Prophet (s) had come to implement in society in front of the King of Abyssinia, the land where a group of early Muslims had fled due to the persecution of Quraysh:

> "O King, we were a people in a state of ignorance and immorality, worshipping idols and eating

> the flesh of dead animals, committing all sorts of abomination and shameful deeds, breaking the ties of kinship, treating guests badly, and the strong among us exploited the weak. We remained in this state until God sent us a Prophet, one of our own people whose lineage, truthfulness, trustworthiness, and integrity were well-known to us. He called us to worship God alone and to renounce the stones and the idols which we and our ancestors used to worship besides God. He commanded us to speak the truth, to honor our promises, to be kind to our relations, to be helpful to our neighbors; to cease all forbidden acts, to abstain from bloodshed, to avoid obscenities and false witness; to not appropriate an orphan's property nor slander chaste women. He ordered us to worship God alone and not to associate anything with Him, to uphold prayer, to give charity and to fast in the month of Ramadan. We believed in him and what he brought to us from God, and we follow him in what he has asked us to do and we keep away from what he forbade us from doing."[1]

Prophet Muḥammad (s) displayed the trait of mercy in its most superior human form:

> "There has come to you a Messenger from among yourselves; grievous to him is your suffering, [ardently] anxious over you, to the believers gentle [and] merciful." (Quran 9:128)

1. Retrieved from https://mydailydeen.com/2019/06/15/the-eloquence-of-jafar-ibn-abi-talib/.

> "So, by mercy from God, [O Muḥammad], you were lenient with them. And if you had been rude [in speech] and harsh in heart, they would have disbanded from around you."(Quran 3:159)

Prophet Muḥammad (s) displayed the highest compassion toward his family members and followers. He expressed affection to the young and the old, and even toward animals. The narrations which relate the mercy of Prophet Muḥammad (s) are so numerous that they can be gathered in an independent book. Not only did Prophet Muḥammad (s) show mercy to the believers, he also displayed deep concern for the disbelievers who rejected his call to monotheism. His sorrow reached a degree that God addressed him in the Quran, saying:

> "So do not let your soul waste away in regrets for them; surely God is Knowing of what they do." (Quran 35:8)

In what follows we shall mention two instances which demonstrate Prophet Muḥammad's (s) compassion. One of the most painful incidents in the life of Prophet Muḥammad (s) was the martyrdom of his beloved and courageous paternal uncle, Ḥamza. Ḥamza had embraced Islam early on and defended the Prophet (s) against the harassment of the idolaters. During the Battle of Uḥud, Prophet Muḥammad (s) sustained an injury on his head and many Muslims were martyred, among them the Prophet's uncle Hamza. Despite his pain and suffering, Prophet Muḥammad (s) prayed for the pagans of Mecca who had come to attack the Muslims, saying: "My God, forgive my people for they do not know."[1]

Years after the battle of Uhud, the pagans of Mecca were vanquished and Prophet Muḥammad (s) entered his home city victorious. He had fled from Mecca eight years before with a single companion, but now he returned at the head of a Muslim army which numbered thousands. It is known that victors often seek retribution against their foes, but Prophet Muḥammad (s) displayed mercy toward the pagans of Mecca who had oppressed and tortured his followers: "We witness his grandness during the Conquest of Mecca. The effects of past torments he was inflicted with could have very well actuated in him feelings of revenge. But Muḥammad (s) prevented his army from shedding even a drop of blood. Showing a majestic compassion, all he did was thank God."[2]

Compassion is a divine attribute beautifully displayed by Prophet Muḥammad (s), and as Muslims we are expected to follow the example of our beloved Prophet (s). In the basmala, we mention God's attributes of mercy, and should actively demonstrate these qualities in our individual and social lives. Each one of us has a spiritual journey to undertake and advancement on this path is not possible without God's grace.

Begin your spiritual ascent with the basmala. Recite it with a devoted heart and a firm resolution. Your existence is a gift of God, and every breath you take is a divine

1. Qadri, Muḥammad Tahir. Muḥammad the Merciful. Minhaj Publications: 2014, p.13.
2. Topbaş, Osman Nuri. The Exemplar Beyond Comparison. Erkam Publications: 2016, p.35.

grace. The path is long, and the obstacles are numerous, but remember that you will always be enveloped by the mercy of your Lord: "One's being, graced continuously by the practice of the basmala, takes on a beautiful fragrance. Just as a mirror cannot help but reflect an image, the sincere aspirant cannot help but be perfumed by the fragrance of divine compassion."[1]

1. Out of Darkness, Into Light, p.149.

Chapter Two:
Boundless Praise

ٱلْحَمْدُ لِلَّهِ رَبِّ ٱلْعَالَمِينَ ﴿٢﴾

2. [All] praise is [due] to Allah, Lord of the worlds –

After opening Sūrat al-Fātiḥa with the basmala, we turn to God in praise reciting: "Praise be to God, Lord of the Worlds". Al-ḥamd is translated into "praise", but this word denotes two meanings in Arabic: an expression of extolment or an offering of gratitude. The formula of praise is a perpetual experience in the lives of Muslims; not only do we recite it in Sūrat al-Fātiḥa but we frequently mention it in our everyday lives as well. When asked, "How are you?", Muslims frequently answer "Praise be to God," even if they are going through hard circumstances.

Al-ḥamd is only expressed to God since He is the source of all favors. Even though you might admire a certain individual for a particular trait or accomplishment, or express thanks[1] to someone who performs an act of kindness toward you, al-ḥamd is limited to God. "We give praise

1. Expressing gratitude to fellow humans is an ethical requirement; for instance, God urges us to be thankful to our parents: "And We have enjoined on man (to be dutiful) to his parents. His mother bore him in weakness upon weakness, and his weaning is in two

on account of some particular praiseworthy achievements or qualities; we feel gratitude for some particular good done. But in relation to God, ḥamd affirms that God is eternally worthy of praise and gratitude because He is God eternally, eternally Merciful, and the Lord of all creation."[1] Hence, the two meanings are merged into one, and the term denotes praising God for his lofty attributes and simultaneously offering thanks to Him for every grace.

> "And whatever favor you have, it is from God." (Quran 16:53)

This may explain why the word al-ḥamd accompanies the word Rabb (Lord). Rabb means the director of the universe and the affairs of mankind, and thus al-ḥamd is expressed to Him who showers us with blessings and manages our affairs. A ḥadīth transmitted from Prophet Muḥammad (s) states that: "When you say, 'Praise be to God, Lord of the Worlds,' you will have thanked God and He [will] increase [your bounty]."[2]

All causal chains are linked to God, and this signifies that the blessings we receive through various means are ultimately traced back to Him. Every source of comfort and joy in life; each heartbeat and every breath we take is a divine blessing. God's graces envelop us during every moment of our lives, even though most humans don't

---

years. Give thanks to Me and to your parents, to me (is your final) destination." (Quran 31:14)

1. Ünal, Ali. The Qur'an with Annotated Interpretation in Modern English. Tughra Books: 2008, p.4.
2. The Study Quran, p.69.

contemplate the ultimate Cause behind them. Thus, al-ḥamd belongs to God, as every single blessing in our lives is a divine endowment: "It should be noted that all praise and thanks are due to God alone, and are His alone. Wherever beauty, excellence and perfection occur, the ultimate source is God. No created beings, whether angels or humans, heavenly or earthly objects, have anything other than a dependent excellence, beauty or perfection. Where these qualities occur, they are, in reality, simply favors from God. Thus, if there is one to whom we should feel indebted and grateful, it is the Creator of everything."[1]

We repeat the verse "Praise be to God, Lord of the Worlds" in every prayer, but it is necessary to ponder the profound meanings this verse conveys.

GRAMMATICAL STRUCTURE

A question may arise: Why is the noun form of "praise" used and not the subject-verb form "I praise" in this holy verse? This may be clarified taking the following points into consideration. The attribution of praise to God by using the noun form removes any emphasis on one's self and signifies that God is deserving of praise unconditionally. The subject-verb form, however, would be connected to the person offering praise or to the moment of articulation, and this would imply a personal and temporal restriction.

Furthermore, humans are not able to count all of God's graces and are not able to fathom God's majesty,

1. The Qur'an with Annotated Interpretation in Modern English, p.4-5.

and thus individual expressions of praise remain lacking. This is why the noun form expresses fixed praise which is not reliant on space or time, and is not contingent on deficient human awareness. This is implied in the following supplication, translated into the spirit of the original: "Praise is for You, in night when it envelops, and praise is for You in daytime when it unfolds, and praise is for You in the hereafter and the first [life]."

WHY IS THE WORD RABB (LORD) USED AND NOT ANOTHER DIVINE NAME?

The word Rabb means the Sustainer and Manager of affairs, and this word encompasses a number of Divine attributes which point to God's providence such as the Giver, Healer, and Provider. Hence, praise is offered to the "Lord of the Worlds" who guides, provides sustenance, heals, and manages the affairs of His creatures. God is Rabb "in that He nurtures the creation that He has brought into being"[1]. This aspect of God's active direction of human affairs is indicated in the Quran in the declaration of Abraham:

> "He said: 'Do you observe that which you have been worshipping,
> You and your ancient forefathers?
> Indeed, they are enemies to me, except the Lord of the Worlds,
> Who created me, and it is He Who guides me,
> And it is He who feeds me and gives me drink,
> And when I am ill, it is He who cures me,

1. Islamic Studies, p.686.

> And who will cause me to die and then bring me to life,
> And who I hope will forgive me my sin on the Day of Judgement." (Quran 26:75-82)

Lordship may be categorized into two classifications: lordship over creation, and lordship which pertains to the divine legislation of laws. The former is manifest through the creation of the universe and the continuance of its divine sustainment, while the second is reflected in God's ordainment of laws which ensure the prosperity of mankind. There is a link between the two forms of lordship; God who brought forth creation into existence possesses all-encompassing knowledge and thus ordains the most appropriate laws for his servants to follow.[1]

"Does He not know, He that created?" (Quran 67:14)

Imagine a lonely traveler who is traversing a risky desert at night with no means of survival. After long and

1. To provide guidance to humans and make divine decrees known, God sent messengers to various communities. These prophetic missions, however, were met by the obstinate rejection of tyrannical rulers who were unwilling to relinquish their privilege or their domineering grip over the masses. Monotheistic religions which preach social justice, promote ethical guidelines, and condemn oppression are always a threat to despots. This is why rulers such as Nimrod and Pharaoh rejected the missions of Abraham and Moses respectively. As lordship means the direction of human affairs, we may understand why Pharaoh said: "I am your highest lord!" (Quran 79:24), indicating his desire to dominate his subjects and enforce his hegemony. The pagans of Mecca were also aware of God being the Creator of the universe, but they were not ready to accept divine authority over them and adhere to God's laws.

exhausting efforts, he suddenly glimpses a beam of light on the horizon. Without it, he would have perished. In a similar manner, divine laws remove mankind from darkness into the light. This entails a heartfelt extolment of God: 'Praise be to God, Lord of the Worlds'.

WHAT DOES THE TERM 'ĀLAMĪN DENOTE?

It is noteworthy that when God describes Himself as Rabb al-'Ālamīn (Lord of the Worlds), He uses the plural form of the noun "world" instead of the singular. How can this be explained?

Two main interpretations of 'ālamīn can be identified. According to the first interpretation, 'ālamīn denotes all created species and objects. This includes humans, animals, plants, and everything else which is created in the universe, from the smallest atom to the largest planet. It also encompasses both the visible and invisible worlds. A ḥadīth transmitted from Imam 'Alī (as) states that 'ālamīn refers to created communities/groups, whether animate or inanimate.[1] Hence, Rabb al-'Ālamīn means the "Sustainer of all the worlds in the whole universe, both the microcosm and the macrocosm, and all beings."[2] Evidence on this may be derived from the Quran. When Pharaoh asked Moses: "And what is Rabb al-'Ālamīn?", Moses replied:

> "Lord of the heavens and the earth and all that is between them, if you had sure belief." (Quran 26:24)

1. Biḥār al-Anwār. Volume 26, p.274.
2. Kazim, Ebrahim. Scientific Commentary of Suratul Fateḥah. Pharos Publishing: 2010, p.63.

As for the second interpretation, 'ālamīn refers to the worlds of rational beings exclusively, whether it is the visible world of humans or the invisible worlds of the jinns and the angels. Sayyed Muḥammad Ḥusayn Ṭabāṭabā'ī "looks at the context of the Fātiḥa to find support for the interpretation of 'ālamīn as referring to the rational beings: the expression Rabb al-'Ālamīn is included in a series of verses which enumerate the names of God, and which lead to the name 'Master of the Day of Judgement'. As 'Judgement is reserved for mankind alone, or together with the jinns,...'ālamīn should refer to the worlds of the human beings and the jinns...'."[1]

Proponents of this view may consult the Quran to derive evidence on this. For instance, rational beings are the ones to benefit from the divine warning:

> "Blessed is He who sent down the Criterion upon His servant that he may be a warner to the worlds." (Quran 25:1)

Additionally, the Quran mentions how God chose the Virgin Mary over all women:

> "And [mention] when the angels said, 'O Mary, indeed God has chosen you and purified you and chosen you above the women of the worlds.'" (Quran 3:42)

The Quran also mentions that God made Mary and Jesus a sign for the worlds. It helps to remember here that rational beings are the ones to understand God's signs:

1. "'Tafsīr' of 'Ālamīn' in 'Rabb Al-Ālamīn'", p.56.

> "And [mention] the one who guarded her chastity, so We breathed into her of Our spirit, and We made her and her son a sign for the worlds." (Quran 21:91)

Thus, the usage of ālamīn to refer to rational beings gains precedence in certain instances.

GRATITUDE TO GOD FOR GUIDANCE TO FAITH

Sūrat al-Fātiḥa vibrates with praise to God after mention of the two forms of His mercy, all-inclusive mercy and specific mercy. It is a divine blessing that among the billions of people all over the globe who are not Muslim and who do not pray, God has guided you to His religion and opened the way for you to pray humbly to him:

> "They consider it a favor upon you that they have embraced Islam. Say, 'Do not consider your Islam a favor upon me. Rather, God has conferred favor upon you that He has guided you to the Faith, if you are truthful.'" (Quran 49:17)

This point is clarified in a letter which Imam 'Alī (as) penned to his son Imam Ḥasan (as): "And know that He Who owns the treasuries of the heavens and of the earth has permitted you to [offer] supplication and has guaranteed the answer [of your supplication]. He has commanded you to ask Him in order that He may give you, and to seek His mercy in order that He may have mercy on you. He has not placed anyone between you and Him that may veil you from Him, and He has not [compelled] you to resort to one who mediates for you to Him. If you err, He has not prevented you from repentance."[1]

A significant cause for praise is that God has not placed a veil between Himself and His servants, and has permitted them to entreat Him and sincerely dedicate themselves to Him. A supplication of Imam 'Alī al-Sajjād (as) states: "He who travels toward you [will traverse] a short distance. You do not veil yourself from your creatures, [but it is their] deeds [which] veil them from you."[2] A supplication recited every night in the holy month of Ramadan -the month of spirituality and divine acceptance of prayers- states: "Praise be to God who answers me when I call upon him, and covers all my faults while I disobey Him."[3]

The spiritual contentment which arises from possessing a bond with God is beyond description. It may be likened to a light which permeates your being and illuminates your heart. Expressing devotion to God and attaching yourself earnestly to Him are the greatest joys. The Sufi female poet, Rābi'a al-'Adawiyya, expressed praise to God for allowing her to form a bond with Him in a poem which is still cited in modern times:

> "I have loved Thee with two loves-
> a selfish love and a love that is worthy of Thee.
> As for the love which is selfish,
> Therein I occupy myself with Thee,
> to the exclusion of all others.
> But in the love which is worthy of Thee,
> Thou dost raise the veil that I may see Thee.

1. Nahj al-Balāghah, p.505-506.
2. Al-Qomī. 'Abbās. Mafātīḥ al-Jinān. Du'ā Abū Ḥamza al-Thamālī.
3. Ibid., Du'ā al-Iftitāḥ.

> Yet is the praise not mine in this or that,
> But the praise is to Thee in both that and this."[1]

With a devout heart and a humble spirit, express your gratitude to God who has guided you to the true Faith, and remember how one day in the past the Muslims were a persecuted minority. Prophet Muḥammad (s) and the early Muslims offered many sacrifices and endured hardship for Islam to reach us safe and sound. When you stand to pray to God in this modern era and express your devotion, remember that for Islam to reach us many Muslims were martyred, sustained physical wounds, bore torture, wept, toiled, and endured pain with strength and determination –all for the sake of God. Contemplate the following incident, for instance.

Prophet Muḥammad (s) unceasingly struggled to deliver God's Message and stood firm in the face of the pagans of Quraysh who mistreated him, rejected his call, and harassed his followers. Finding the people of Mecca unresponsive, Prophet Muḥammad (s) journeyed to the city of Ṭā'if, southeast of Mecca, to call its inhabitants to abandon their idol-worship, but he was met with discourtesy by the chieftains of the city. They did not even let him depart in peace and set slaves and fools in the city after him to throw stones at him. He was pelted with rocks to the extent that his feet bled and his shoes were smeared with blood. This did not cause him to lose his determination, and he persevered along with his followers so that the Message of God could reach humanity. In a few years' time, the patience and continuous struggle of

1. Retrieved from https://www.goodreads.com/quotes/7267046-love-i-have-loved-thee-with-two-loves--a.

Prophet Muḥammad (s) and the Muslims reaped results and Islam became the dominant religion in the Arabian Peninsula.

GRATITUDE TO GOD FOR THE CONFERMENT OF FAVORS

If you contemplate the phases of your life, from early infancy to childhood and adulthood, you will realize that in every single moment of your life you have received endowments from God, whether perceptible or imperceptible.

> "And if you count the favors of God, you cannot number them. Indeed, God is Forgiving and Merciful." (Quran 16:18)

God's graces envelop you from the moment you wake up in the morning and throughout the day, when you rest your head on your pillowcase and during your slumber. We often take life's blessings for granted: our sharp mental capacities and sound physical abilities, the roof over our head, the running water in our homes, enough food on the table, social security, accessibility to medical care, and the presence of our loved ones safe and healthy around us. All of the graces we enjoy require constant gratitude, but it is striking that God says in the Holy Quran:

> "And few of My servants are grateful." (Quran 34:13)

Expression of gratitude is in itself a divine favor. The Quran relates a supplication of the Prophet Solomon in which he asks God to enable him to show gratitude:

> "My Lord, enable me to be grateful for Your favor which You have bestowed upon me and upon my parents, and to do righteousness of which You approve. And admit me by Your mercy into [the ranks of] Your righteous servants." (Quran 27:19)

Solomon was king over the magnificent city of Jerusalem, with armies of humans, jinns, and birds at his command. He effectively ruled a prosperous kingdom, but was never unmindful of offering gratitude to God. Solomon's prayer and righteous conduct distinguished him from worldly rulers who reveled in ostentatious wealth and denied God's favor upon them. It is also worth noting that Solomon asked God to enable him to offer gratitude not only for the favor God granted him, but for that which God had bestowed upon his parents as well. This may be explained taking into account that many of the blessings that people receive are an extension of the blessings which God had granted to their parents before them, such as a religious upbringing, robust health and favorable financial circumstances.

Familiarity with blessings might cause us to forget to offer gratitude to God, but when we see the misfortunes of others this should awaken us to express gratitude. A ḥadīth transmitted from Prophet Muḥammad (s) states that: "If you see people [afflicted with] tribulation, then praise God [but] do not let them overhear it because it saddens them."[1] Another ḥadīth transmitted from Imam Ja'far al-Ṣādiq (as) advises a person who sees someone with a deformity, or someone who has a severed organ due to torture, or someone who is afflicted with tribulation

1. Biḥār al-Anwār. Volume 90, p.218.

to secretly say to himself thrice: "Praise be to God who has exempted me from what He has tested you, and if he wanted he would have done that to me."[1]

The following supplication, translated in the spirit of the original, serves in awakening the reader to the blessings God has bestowed upon him/her, and to offer sincere praise:

> "My God, many a living being suffers the constant agony of death, day in, day out, and hears the rattling sound passing through his gasping throat. What he stands face to face with makes his heart tremble with fear, and a cold feverish shivering runs through his body, but I am kept free from this terrible experience.
>
> My God, many a living being is ailing, day in, day out, suffering pain, on the threshold of death, restless and crying in anguish, finding no relief. Neither food nor drink pass easily down his throat, both are tasteless, but I am safe and sound, living a peaceful and easy life, on account of Your kind attention and care.
>
> My God and Master, many a living being is oppressed and kept prisoner, day after day, under the harsh control of ruthless enemies and infidels, separated from his family and children, cut off from his friends and home, imagining how death will come, and how torture will beset him, but I am safe from all this.

1. Ibid., p.217.

> My God, many a living being, day in, day out, drifts over the perilous seas, in the midst of terrifying hurricanes and surging waves, sure of death by drowning, yet is unable to attain safety. There are others who are hit by lightning, or buried alive under destroyed buildings, or consumed by fire, or thrown into deep waters, or suffocated, or drowned, or emaciated, or stoned to death. But I am safe from all this.
>
> So praise be to Thee, O Lord, in [Thy] invulnerable Omnipotence, and prudent Forbearance. Bless Muḥammad (s) and the family of Muḥammad (s), and let me be among those who thank Thee for Thy bounties and remember Thee for Thy favors."[1]

A GRATEFUL HEART

Gratitude is a component of praise: "An integral part of praising God is the expression of gratitude, a practice that just happens to be a primary technique to attain happiness and fulfilment in life. 'Whatever is in the heavens and on earth glorifies God,' says the Quran (62:1), and by joining the cosmic chorus we move our personalities into alignment with all of creation. The Holy Book urges us to grow in this essential practice. 'So which of the favors of your Lord do you deny?' it asks repeatedly, and it reminds

1. Islamic Duas: A Compilation of Prayers (compiled by Duas.Org), p.5-7.

us that if we were to count God's blessings, we could never compute them."[1]

Hence, a believer must always have a grateful heart. "Generosity blossoms in the soil of gratitude. The more aware and grateful we are for our blessings, the more open-hearted and generous our hearts become. The Quran shows us that we experience God's generosity through our gratitude: 'If you are grateful, I will surely give you more' (14:7). Since what you focus on or magnify becomes bigger, when you focus on your blessings, you find more for which to be grateful."[2]

WHEN SHOULD WE OFFER PRAISE TO GOD?

Scholars mention that it is mustaḥab (religiously recommended) to perform sujūd (prostration) and offer thanks to God in several instances such as: the renewal of a blessing, the avoidance of misfortune, the fulfillment of an obligation or the performance of an act of benevolence. Prostration is also recommended when one remembers a previous grace, even if it had occurred months or years previously.

It is unfortunate that many humans fall into heedlessness. The familiarity with numerous blessings sometimes causes people to overlook them or to appreciate them only when they are lost:

---

1. Out of Darkness, Into Light, p.173.
2. Helwa, A. Secrets of Divine Love: A Spiritual Journey into the Heart of Islam. Naulit: 2020.

> "And whatever favor you have, it is from God. Then, when misfortune touches you, to Him you cry for help." (Quran 16:53)

Sūrat al-Fātiḥa teaches us that praise should be offered to God unceasingly. This is reflected in other Quranic verses:

- Noah and Salvation:

  "And when you have boarded the ship, you and those with you, then say, 'Praise be to God who has saved us from the wrongdoing people.'" (Quran 23:28)

- Abraham Gaining Offspring in Old Age:

  "Praise to God, who has granted to me in old age Ismail and Isaac. Indeed, my Lord is the Hearer of supplication." (Quran 14:39)

- Divine Favor upon David and Solomon:

  "And We certainly gave David and Solomon knowledge, and they said, 'Praise be to God who has favored us over many of His believing servants." (Quran 27:15)

  "And say, 'Praise be to God. He will show you His signs, so you will recognize them. And your Lord is not unaware of what you do." (Quran 27:93)

HOW SHOULD WE OFFER PRAISE?

Through Quranic verses, we may notice a contradiction between gratitude and disbelief. Ingratitude is a reflection of the denial and rejection of God's blessings.

> "And when your Lord proclaimed, 'If you are thankful, I will surely increase you [in favor]; but if you deny, indeed, My punishment is severe.'" (Quran 14:7)

> "If you disbelieve -indeed, God has no need of you. And He does not approve for His servants disbelief. And if you are thankful, He approves it for you." (Quran 39:7)

Ingratitude is the refusal to acknowledge good, and therefore it is a moral failure. Gratefulness is not merely a swift expression of gratitude which a person articulates without concentration, but it involves several levels. The first is awareness: to know that each favor you enjoy -whether apparent or subtle, obvious or concealed- is a blessing from God. This is followed by the second level, a deep feeling of reverence which arises from knowing that all blessings are a gift from God, and that no grace reaches you independently of Him. The third level involves the overflow of gratitude from your heart to your tongue. Hence, the verbal expression of praise in Sūrat al-Fātiḥa should be joined with a sincere and conscious feeling of gratitude.

A ḥadīth transmitted from Imam Ja'far al-Ṣādiq (as) states that thankfulness is complete when one says: Praise be to God, Lord of the Worlds.[1] The following account further illustrates the significance of praising God. Imam Ja'far al-Ṣādiq (as) exited from the mosque one day, but he noticed that his mount was lost, so he pledged: "If God returns it to me, I shall thank God with thanks due to Him." His mount was soon found and returned to him, and the Imam said: "Al-ḥamdulilah (Praise be to God)." One of those present was surprised when he heard this short phrase, as he was expecting a more elaborate expression. This drove him to remark: "May I be sacrificed for you. Did you not say: 'I shall thank God with thanks due to Him'?" Imam Ja'far al-Ṣādiq (as) answered: "Did you not hear me say: 'Al-ḥamdulilah'?"[2] This phrase which Imam Ja'far al-Ṣādiq (as) uttered was short in length, but as it sprang from a grateful heart that was aware of the bounty of God, it was an expression of true and deep gratitude.

The three phases of gratitude -awareness, heartfelt reverence, and oral expression- are never complete without action. The requirement to perform actions out of gratitude is indicated in the following verse:

> "Work, O family of David, in gratitude. And few of My servants are grateful." (Quran 34:13)

Perhaps the interpretation of the second phrase in the aforementioned verse is that many people restrict gratitude to speech without translating it into action, and in this way gratitude remains deficient. Divine favors place a responsibility upon the individual to act according to God's commands and employ all favors as God wishes. It

1. Al-Kāfī. Volume 2, p.95.
2. Ibid., p.97.

is recounted that Prophet Muḥammad (s) used to stand in prayer until his feet swelled. When he was asked why, he answered, "Shall I not be a grateful servant?"[1]

In Sūrat al-Fātiḥa, God teaches us how to praise him: "This is praise of the lovingly kind God, the Creator who provides daily provisions, the One in name and mark... He saw the servants' incapacity to recognize His measure, and He knew that as much as they tried, they would not arrive... In the perfection of His exaltedness, majesty, and holiness, He made [humans] His deputies in laudation of Him, taught them how to praise Him, and gave them permission to do so. Otherwise, who would dream of saying 'Praise belongs to God' if He had not said it Himself? Who in the whole world would have the gall to say, 'Praise belongs to God'?"[2]

Revive your heart of clay with humble praise: "Praise be to God, Lord of the Worlds". You are a recipient of God's blessings in every second of your life -even now while you are reading these words- despite the fact that you might not always be attentive to this reality. Praise belongs to God for what he has bestowed upon you, and praise belongs to God for His gentle care and His encompassing love. Live by this verse, and end all your affairs with it, and know that it will accompany you in this worldly life and the hereafter.

When God relates the state of the believers in Heaven who have done virtuous deeds, He says:

1. Borūjerdī, Hussein. Jāme' Aḥadīth al-Shī'a. Volume 5, p.84.
2. The Unveiling of the Mysteries and the Provision of the Pious, p.23.

"Their prayer therein will be: 'Glory be to You, O God!' And their greeting therein will be: 'Peace'. And the conclusion of their prayer will be: 'Praise be to God, Lord of the Worlds.'" (Quran 10:10)

Chapter Three:
Overflowing Mercy

ٱلرَّحْمَٰنِ ٱلرَّحِيمِ ﴿٣﴾

3. The Compassionate, the Merciful.

It is noteworthy that the two divine attributes -ar-Raḥmān and ar-Raḥīm- are repeated twice in Sūrat al-Fātiḥa, in the first and the third verse. This repetition serves an important purpose as it stresses the significance of these two divine attributes.

Raḥma is an Arabic word which means mercy. Mercy prompts a person to offer good to another, and this act of kindness is not performed in return for something, but is done out of compassion. It is worth noting that the word raḥem, the Arabic word for "womb", is closely linked to raḥma: "The connection in the Arabic language between the womb and the concept of mercy is clear in both form and meaning. The Arabic root raḥima, 'to be merciful,' produces the noun raḥma, 'mercy,' and the divine names, ar-Raḥmān, the Merciful, and ar-Raḥīm, the Compassionate, which open almost every sūra of the Quran. The same root produces the word raḥem, "womb". This powerful linking of terms stresses the sacredness of the womb and provides a strong justification for the respect given to mothers in Islam... The love and care that a mother extends toward her children is a reflection of the loving mercy of God toward all of His creatures."[1]

REFLECTIONS ON THIS QURANIC VERSE:

1. The mention of the two divine attributes ar-Raḥmān and ar-Raḥīm, before and after the verse "Praise be to God, Lord of the Worlds", stresses divine mercy. The Holy Quran makes it clear that mercy is the reason of creation:

   "Except on whom your Lord has mercy, and for that He created them." (Quran 11:119)

   "My mercy encompasses all things." (Quran 7:156)

   Therefore, God's mercy should drive a person to offer praise to God.

2. The all-inclusive mercy of God (indicated by ar-Raḥmān) is mentioned before the exclusive mercy which is granted to the believers (indicated by ar-Raḥīm). This signifies that all creatures are initially encompassed by divine mercy, even humans who are sinful or heedless of God. The second reference to unique mercy signifies that humans can work to attain a special form of mercy, and thus become enveloped by two divine mercies. Both of these mercies are cause for praise.

---

1. Cornell, Vincent J. (General Editor). Voices of Islam: Voices of Life: Family, Home, and Society. Praeger Publishers: 2007, p.87.

3. The divine attributes ar-Raḥmān and ar-Raḥīm which are mentioned twice in Sūrat al-Fātiḥa are mentioned other times in the Quran:

   "And your God is One God; there is no god but He, the Compassionate, the Merciful." (Quran 2:163)

   "He is God; other than whom there is no god. He is the Knower of the Unseen and the Visible; He is the Compassionate, the Merciful." (Quran 59:22)

   This highlights the importance of Sūrat al-Fātiḥa which carries a key to mercy.

4. The first verse which mentions the two attributes of divine mercy is followed by the verse: "Praise be to God, Lord of the Worlds", while the verse which includes a repetition of these attributes is followed by: "Master of the Day of Judgement". The first verse may point to God's mercy which is manifest in bringing the universe into existence while the third verse may be an indication of divine mercy which shall be manifest on Judgement Day.

THE MOST-MERCIFUL OF THE MERCIFUL

The derivatives of raḥma have been mentioned frequently in the Quran. God brought the universe into existence through His mercy, and continues to sustain it and its inhabitants through His mercy. It is true that humans display mercy toward one another –and this is evident through acts of kindness, cooperation and charity- but the mercy of all human beings combined may never be compared to divine mercy.

> "Say: If you possessed the treasuries of my Lord's mercy, you would withhold out of fear of spending; and man is [ever] niggardly." (Quran 17:100)

From this, we may understand why the epithet "The Most-Merciful of the Merciful" only applies to God. This designation is mentioned numerous times in the Quran:

- In Jacob's speech to his sons:

  "He said, 'Should I entrust you with him except as I entrusted you with his brother before? But God is the best Guardian, and He is the Most-Merciful of the merciful.'" (Quran 12:64)

- In Joseph's speech to his brothers:

  "He said, 'No blame will there be upon you today. God will forgive you; and He is the Most-Merciful of the merciful.'" (Quran 12:92)

- In Moses's prayer:

  "He said: 'My Lord, forgive me and my brother and admit us into Your mercy, and You are the Most-Merciful of the merciful.'" (Quran 7:151)

- In Job's prayer:

  "And [mention] Job, when he cried to his Lord, 'Indeed, adversity has touched me, and you are the Most-Merciful of the merciful.'" (Quran 21:83)

God's mercy teaches us to actively display mercy in our lives: "God has led people by example in offering us His unconditional mercy. Through the prophets and His Word, as well as through our human disposition to make God the center of our lives, God has granted us the opportunity to accept His mercy by living it ourselves and passing it on...We are called to show mercy in our actions in the here and now; our actions are the logical reaction to the mercy God has shown us. By denying others our mercy, we exclude ourselves from God's mercy; we reject God's mercy. Our love for God must manifest itself in the active showing of mercy within society. This vocation, calling us to show mercy in our interactions with others, represents the key message of Islamic ethos."[1]

God possesses absolute attributes; His knowledge, power, and mercy encompass all things. A report describes how Imam Ja'far al-Ṣādiq (as) used to offer sujūd and say: "Yā arḥam ar-Rāḥimīn" (O' the Most-Merciful of the merciful) seven times before asking God to fulfill his need. It is also reported that Imam 'Alī al-Sajjād (as) was once told that Ḥasan al-Basrī, a renown theologian and ascetic, had expressed amazement at how a person will be saved in the afterlife in view of the strictness in reckoning. To this, Imam 'Alī al-Sajjād (as) remarked that it is not strange how one will be saved, rather it is strange how one could perish with the vastness of God's mercy!

The human fitra contributes to directing humans toward God, the Most-Merciful of the merciful. It is recounted that a man asked Imam Ja'far al-Ṣādiq (as) about God. The Imam (as) asked him if he had ever been on board a stricken ship with no aid in sight and where swimming would be of no avail. When the man answered in the affirmative, Imam Ja'far al-Ṣādiq (as) asked him if

1. Khorchide, Mouhanad; Hartmann, Sarah. Islam is Mercy: Essential Features of a Modern Religion. Herder: 2014.

his heart had clung to something which would save him from his predicament. When the man confirmed this, Imam Ja'far al-Ṣādiq (as) clarified that the savior the man's heart had clung to was God –the one who is able to save when there is no savior, and to give succor when there is no succorer.[1]

1. Biḥār al-Anwār, volume 64, p.137.

Chapter Four: **Majestic Sovereignty**

مَٰلِكِ يَوْمِ ٱلدِّينِ ۝٤

4. Master of the Day of Judgement.

Thus verse serves to alert humans to their everlasting fate and awakens a mixture of feelings in them: fear and hope. The former arises from humility toward God and awareness of the magnitude of Judgement Day, while the second arises from knowledge of God's mercy and awareness of the salvation of believers who perform righteous deeds. This verse inspires a person with a sense of responsibility over his/her every word and action because all humans will inevitably be held accountable on Judgement Day.

> "Do they not think that they will be resurrected,
> For a tremendous Day,
> The Day when mankind shall stand before the Lord of the Worlds." (Quran 83:3-5)

The Quran describes Judgement Day in striking images; for instance, the immensity of that day is indicated in the following verse:

> "Then how, if you disbelieve, will you protect yourselves from a day which shall make children grey-headed?" (Quran 73:17)

The Quran also clarifies that every person will receive a book which contains an account of his/her deeds in the worldly life. This should inspire every believer to prepare for that day and fill his/her record with righteous actions. As long as you are alive, you have the chance to repent to your Lord, make amends, and fill your book with virtuous actions.

> "And [for] every person We have imposed his ṭā'er (deeds) upon his neck, and We will produce for him on the Day of Resurrection a book which he shall encounter spread open.
> 'Read your book! Your soul suffices you this day as a reckoner against you.'" (Quran 17:13-14)

Belief in Judgement Day confers meaning on human life. Every human being possesses an instinct of self-preservation and innately recoils from the idea of a permanent cessation of being and the separation from loved ones after a life spent vibrantly in various pursuits and occupations. Belief in the afterlife inspires humans with hope and fulfills their instinct of self-preservation. It also invokes a sense of responsibility which accompanies the realization of future accountability. You will be asked about your intentions, your conduct, your words. Did you fulfill the obligations God imposed upon you and refrain from religious prohibitions? Did you benefit from your time or waste it in sins and trivialities? Did you conduct your transactions legitimately and avoid prohibited dealings such as fraud and bribery? How did you amass your wealth and how did you spend it? Did you raise your children in a proper manner? Did you act with kindness and manners toward others, or were you unkind to them?

We will be asked about all details concerning our lives. Thus, the conscious recitation of the verse "Master of the Day of Judgement" contributes to self-rectification when accompanied by active determination and action.

REFLECTIONS ON THE VERSE:

1. In this verse, the Arabic term for Judgement Day is "Yawm ad-Dīn"; with dīn meaning requital (recompense or reckoning). This signifies that conduct is what matters, that external appearances or illustrious ancestry are of no true significance, and that value is given to our deeds:

   > "And you shall not be recompensed except for what you used to do." (Quran 37:39)

   "Yawm ad-Dīn" (Day of Judgement) is mentioned 13 times in the Quran. The word dīn has a number of meanings in Arabic, among them judgement, recompense, and submission. The Divine Name Ad-Dayyān means Judge/Reckoner. The different synonyms may be combined to produce a general meaning that denotes the gathering of mankind in submission to God to be judged for their actions.

2. The Day of Judgement is described as a "day" (yawm), but it is not equivalent to the normal 24-hour day we know which results from the Earth's rotation around

the sun. Bear in mind that on Judgement Day, our solar system will be upturned and the universe as we know it will be significantly changed. Therefore, the rotations and orbits in the universe which cause days, months, and years will not be in effect anymore.

> "The angels and the Spirit will ascend to Him during a Day the measure of which is fifty thousand years." (Quran 70:4)

A ḥadīth transmitted from Imam Ja'far al-Ṣādiq (as) states: "Hold yourselves accountable before you are held accountable, for there are fifty stations [on] Resurrection Day, [and] each station's measure is one thousand years." It is transmitted that after saying this, Imam Ja'far al-Ṣādiq (as) recited the aforementioned verse.[1]

3. The verse "The Compassionate, the Merciful" may refer to the divine mercy which is manifest in the creation of the universe, the **beginning**. This is followed by the verse "Master of the Day of Judgement" which expresses God's sovereignty on Resurrection Day, signaling the **end of mortality**. This emphasizes the Divine Names: al-Awwal (The First) and al-'Ākher (The Last), or 'al-Mubdi' (The Originator) and al-Mu'īd (The Restorer/Reviver).

4. God's sovereignty extends over all aspects of existence, but we may state that sovereignty over Judgement Day is specifically mentioned in Sūrat al-Fātiḥa because it is the day when monotheism and divine justice will

1. Al-Ṭabrasī. Majma' al-Bayān. Al-Majma' al-'Ālamī li Taqrīb. Volume 6, p.766.

become manifest to all mankind, and every soul will find itself under the dominion of God.

5. Divine mercy and sovereignty over Judgement Day are mentioned together, for the greatest manifestation of God's mercy will be on that day.

   "True sovereignty, that Day, is for ar-Raḥmān." (Quran 25:26)

   "On that Day, everyone will follow [the call of] the Caller [with] no deviation therefrom, and [all] voices will be hushed before ar-Raḥmān, so you will not hear except a faint sound." (Quran 20:108)

   This link between divine mercy and sovereignty demonstrates that despite the overwhelming sensations which will engulf a person on Judgement Day, God will always be with the believers.

6. Supreme dominion over Judgement Day belongs to God alone. Wealth, material possessions and worldly authority amount to nothing on that day, and personal property will be of no avail. This should drive a person to carefully consider his/her financial dealings and actively seek God's mercy by shunning avarice, paying obligatory alms, donating charity, and ensuring legitimate profit.

RECITATION VARIANTS

This Arabic word for sovereign is recited in two forms: Mālik with a long a, or Malik with a short a. The first variant –Mālik- is derived from the noun milk which denotes possession; thus Mālik means the Possessor. The second variant –Malik- is derived from the word mulk which means authority; thus Malik means the Sovereign or Dominator.

Mulk is mentioned in the Quran to denote worldly authority in the following verses:

> "And Pharaoh called out among his people; he said, 'O my people, does not the **mulk** (kingship) of Egypt belong to me, and these rivers flowing beneath me; then do you not see?" (Quran 43:51)

> "Have you not considered the one who argued with Abraham about his Lord because God had given him **mulk** (kingship)?" (Quran 2:258)

True and encompassing mulk, however, belongs only to God, and all worldly authority of humans will come to an end. Every monarch, king, emperor, and head of state will meet his death.

It is noteworthy that in another Quranic verse, Mālik and mulk are combined in a manner which denotes God's ownership over the entire realm of existence.

> "Say, 'O God, **Mālik al-Mulk** (Owner of Sovereignty), You give **mulk** to whom You will, and You take **mulk** away from whom You will.'" (Quran 3:26)

This verse indicates that God possesses complete sovereignty, and that bestowal of kingship occurs according to His wisdom.

WHY IS SOVEREIGNTY OVER JUDGEMENT DAY SPECIFICALLY MENTIONED IN SŪRAT AL-FĀTIḤA?

God possesses absolute sovereignty over everything, but how can we understand the specific mention in Sūrat al-Fātiḥa of God's dominion over Judgement Day? This may be explained as follows: The worldly life abides by the law of causality –gaining sustenance requires work, healing entails medical treatment, and achievement requires effort. But on Judgement Day, all matters will be directly attributed to God.

Humans will exit from their graves, lacking any wealth or worldly possessions. Bank accounts, valuable property, stocks and real estate –matters which humans hold in high value in the worldly life- will be useless on that day.

> "Their eyes humbled, they will emerge from the graves as if they were scattered locusts." (Quran 54:7)

> "And you have certainly come to Us alone as We created you the first time, and you have left whatever We bestowed upon you behind you." (Quran 6:94)

What truly matters on Judgement Day is the purity of heart:

> "The day on which property will not avail, nor sons. Except him who comes to God with a pure heart." (Quran 26:88-89)

On Judgement Day, humans will be helpless to the extent that they will not be able to exert control even over their own organs:

> "[That] Day, We will seal their mouths, and their hands will speak to Us, and their feet will testify about what they used to earn." (Quran 36:65)

> The Quran further states that the disbelievers will be called to prostrate themselves before God, but that they will be unable to do so (Quran 68:42).

On that day, the wrongdoers will wish to spend all that is on earth to save themselves:

> "And if those who did wrong had all that is in the earth entirely and the like of it with it, they would [attempt to] ransom themselves therewith from the awful punishment on the Day of Resurrection." (Quran 39:47)

On that Day of great magnitude, sovereignty is for God alone:

> "The Day they come forth, nothing concerning them will be concealed from God. To whom belongs **mulk** (sovereignty) this Day? To God, the One, the Prevailing." (Quran 40:16)

NAMES OF JUDGEMENT DAY

The Quran mentions approximately 100 names or descriptive terms for Judgement Day which befit the context of the sūras they are mentioned in. Examples include: The Final Day, The Great Day, The Promised Day, Day of Resurrection, Day of Gathering, Day of Truth, Day of Reckoning, Day of Eternal Life, Day of Rising, Day of Regret, Witnessed Day, and Day of Sorting

Out. This is indicative of the linguistic eloquence of the Quran, as every word represents a certain aspect of the Final Day and inspires the soul with solemnity.

> "The day of every king's empire ends and disappears, his kingship finishes, and his state changes. But God's kingship is permanent, today and tomorrow, for it never comes to an end or disappears. In the two worlds nothing and no one is outside of His kingship and ruling power. No one has a kingship like His kingship. Today He is the Lord of the Worlds and tomorrow the Owner of the Day of Doom, and none of the creatures is like this... How can the servant do anything? For in the two worlds, ownership and kingship are God's, without associate, partner, requirement, or need. So where is the servant's choice? He who has no ownership has no ruling power."[1]

1. The Unveiling of the Mysteries and the Provision of the Pious, p.25.

Chapter Five:

Humble Devotion

إِيَّاكَ نَعْبُدُ وَإِيَّاكَ نَسْتَعِينُ ٥

5. You [alone] do we worship and You [alone] do we ask for aid.

> "As the Earth revolves through one time zone after another, an unceasing wave of Muslims bowing to God turns the planet into a magnificent prayer rug."[1]

God is the originator who brought us forth into existence: "the Compassionate, the Merciful", and to Him we shall return: "Master of the Day of Judgment" to gain a reward for our virtuous actions and to be held accountable for our misdeeds. From birth to death, we are cared for by a Merciful God to whom we shall return.

> "Indeed we belong to Allāh, and indeed to Him we shall return." (Quran 2:156)

Sūrat al-Fātiḥa guides us to declare exclusive worship to God and to request assistance from Him alone: "You [alone] do we worship and You [alone] do we ask for aid".

---

1. Out of Darkness, Into Light, p.169.

We worship Him alone, the Lord of mercy who brought us forth into existence, who gives us hope in an eternal life, and who will ask each one of us about the fulfillment of his/her responsibility in the worldly life.

Worship entails diligence in practice and steadfastness in the face of temptations, and this may only be achieved through divine assistance. To attain the high levels of servitude, we need God's aid. When we address God saying: "You [alone] do we worship and You [alone] do we ask for aid", we express our link to Him. Even though some individuals might verbally repeat this verse without thoughtful observation, it is important to state that with contemplation and repetition, the meaning will reach the heart.

In Sūrat al-Fātiḥa, we express our answer to God's call for us to worship Him and we express our sincere devotion.

> "And that you worship Me. This is a Straight Path." (Quran 36:61)

> "And they were not commanded except to worship God, [being] sincere to Him in religion, ḥunafā' (inclining to truth), and to establish prayer and to give zakah; and that is the right religion." (Quran 98:5)

It is also a response to the calls of the prophets like Hūd, Ṣāleḥ, and Shu'ayb mentioned in various verses in the Quran[1].

1. Quran 7:65, 7:73, 7:85; Quran 11:61; 11:84; Quran 23:23.

> "O my people, worship Allāh; you have no deity other than Him."

We may notice that the first four verses in Sūrat al-Fātiḥa form a doctrinal prelude to this fifth verse, and open the way for a heartfelt declaration of: "You [alone] do we worship and You [alone] do we ask for aid". The soul becomes prepared to express sincere worship and request aid from God alone, and declare its conviction that no creature can be of real benefit without God's permission.

If we consider the positioning of this holy verse within Sūrat al-Fātiḥa, we may notice the following: "This [verse] comes at the center of the passage, and follows logically from the earlier part. Only when the first part has been conceded can the second follow naturally. Who is more worthy of being singled out for worship, and in seeking help, other than the caring Lord of the Worlds, the Lord of Mercy, the Giver of Mercy, the Master of the Day of Judgment? Because there is judgment, the judgment should be prepared for by worship."[1]

REFLECTIONS ON THE HOLY VERSE:

1- It is noteworthy that the verse states: "You [alone] do we worship" and not: "We worship You." The pronoun referring to God ("You") is mentioned before the verb "worship", and when the object is mentioned before the verb this serves in Arabic grammar to emphasize exclusivity. Therefore, the meaning is that worship is offered only to God, and this is known as monotheism

---

1. Understanding the Qur'an: Themes and Style, p.19.

in worship. When we recite Sūrat al-Fātiḥa, our recitation is in harmony with the parts of prayer we are offering. When we turn in the direction of the Sacred Mosque at Mecca, and bow and prostrate to God we are actively and outwardly expressing our belief that worship is due to God alone.

2- This verse expresses true monotheism and the rejection of anything which is "worshipped" other than God. In line with this, it serves as a repudiation of not only idols, but of everything which drives a person away from God such as egoism, whims, personal interests, material possessions, and the affiliation with tyrants. Humans experience a conflict in this world between Truth and falsehood, fitra and deviation, guidance and error, restraint and surrender to the temptations of Satan and the self. The daily recitation of "You [alone] do we worship and You [alone] do we ask for aid" is a declaration of a personal resolve in the battle with temptations. "Worshippers should be fully present before their Lord. Their attention should not be divided between God and something else, either openly, as in idol worship, or secretly, as in the case of those who worship God distracted by thoughts and subjective desires or intent upon personal reward. Rather, one should "worship God, devoting religion [entirely] to Him (39:2)."[1]

3- A grammatical shift is evident in this verse. "In the first three verses of this passage, God is spoken about in the third person. This perspective on God conveys a sense of his majesty and dominance over creation. The fourth

1. Ibid., p.74.

verse then startles the listener/reader with its use of the second person singular to address God; suddenly the relationship becomes intimate and personal. The grammatical shift employed in this passage not only serves a stylistic purpose but also conveys a theological message: that God is in complete command over all of creation, yet in his majesty is immediately accessible to those who turn to Him in worship and supplication."[1]

4- Another grammatical clarification relates to the usage of the plural form "we worship" rather than the singular "I worship". This may guide the believers to the fact that one must be concerned with the collective salvation of the Muslim community and not only personal salvation. This is indicated in a verse which emphasizes that man is in loss "Except those who believe and do righteous deeds, and exhort one another to truth and exhort one another to patience." (Quran 103:3)

God wants the believers to free themselves from egoism and individualism. The faithful are not expected to neglect their personal affairs, but they are also required to take an active part in the Muslim community. From here, we may understand that the verse does not use the first person singular "I worship" because God wants us to free ourselves from our egos and to bear a social responsibility. "Human beings speak here in the first-person plural, hence not only as individuals, but also as vicegerents of God, supplicating God on behalf of all of creation. To speak to God in

1. Mattson, Ingrid. The Story of the Qur'an: Its History and Place in Muslim Life. Wiley-Blackwell: 2013, p.44.

the first-person plural rather than the singular also implies humility before the Divine, both because one is not focused solely upon oneself and because one acknowledges that ultimately only God has the right to say 'I'."[1]

5- The fifth verse of Sūrat al-Fātiḥa mentions the aim (worship) and the means to fulfill it (divine assistance). Both the aim and the means are mentioned in this verse. This signifies that God guides humans to the purpose of their existence -worship- and aids them in its achievement. "The request for God's help can thus be seen as a request for further aid in worshipping and serving Him and in all of one's affairs, a request founded upon the acknowledgement that one is never independent of God and that it is only through His assistance that one can worship Him, not through one's own power and strength."[2]

DIFFERENCE BETWEEN ISTI'ĀNA AND ISTI'ĀTHA

Isti'ātha refers to seeking God's protection from evil, while isti'āna means requesting aid from God, whether in obtaining blessings or warding off evil. In this manner, isti'āna is more general than isti'ātha. For instance, Sūrat al-Falaq and Sūrat al-Nās include isti'āthas from various forms of evil, while in Sūrat al-Fātiḥa the isti'āna -request for aid- is general and encompasses all circumstances and

1. The Study Quran, p.74.
2. Ibid., p.75.

challenges. Just as worship is entitled to God alone, so should assistance be asked only from God.[1]

The request for divine aid alerts a person to the fact that no matter how much physical strength, authority, academic achievement or possessions one amasses, s/he will always remain a humble servant in need of the assistance of his/her Lord. This realization wards off the sense of personal superiority or self-importance.

> "O mankind, you are in need of God, while God is the Self-sufficient, the Praiseworthy." (Quran 35:15)

---

1. An account relates how the Abbasid Caliph al-Mansūr once ordered [his agents] to bring Imam Ja'far al-Ṣādiq to his assembly with the intent of killing him. Someone had informed al-Mansūr of a false report claiming that Imam Ja'far al-Ṣādiq was striving to undermine al-Mansūr's caliphate and that the Imam was plotting against the caliph. When Imam Ja'far al-Ṣādiq denied these reports, al-Mansūr summoned the informant. Imam Ja'far al-Ṣādiq demanded that the informant should swear to God to prove his honesty, but the latter became agitated and his lie was revealed. Imam Ja'far al-Ṣādiq was ultimately saved. The caliph's vizier, al-Rabī', was a friend of the Imam. He asked him one day: "When you entered into the presence of al-Mansūr, he was angry to the extreme, [in a manner whereby] he would not have slackened in killing you. [Meanwhile,] you were moving your lips, and every time you moved your lips the anger of al-Mansūr was calmed. [What were you saying?]" Imam Ja'far al-Ṣādiq answered that he had been reciting the supplication of his grandfather, Hussein son of Ali, and he proceeded to relate the following supplication (translated in the spirit): "O my means at times of hardship! O my aid in times of grievance! Guard me with Your eye which does not sleep, and aid me with Your support which is unopposed."

   Al-Rabī' remarked that he memorized this supplication and recited it when he faced hardships, always finding relief from God.

THE PURPOSE OF EXISTENCE

The Holy Quran clearly states the wisdom behind the creation of the two rational creatures, jinn and humankind:

> "And I did not create the jinn and mankind except to worship Me." (Quran 51:56)

Offering worship to God is therefore an existential purpose which every individual should fulfill. When we recite "You [alone] do we worship", we are responding to God who did not create us in vain but to display servitude to Him. True worship occurs when one obeys his Lord and refrains from acting according to personal whims.

A sincere servant, therefore, reflects the attributes of God in their human form. S/he is compassionate, kind, wise, forgiving, enforces justice, and stands against oppression. It is noteworthy that in the shahāda –the Muslim declaration of faith which is recited during prayer- we mention the servitude of Prophet Muḥammad (s) to God prior to mentioning his rank as a messenger. This emphasizes the importance of servitude which is the essence of prophecy.

> "I testify that there is no god but Allāh,
> and that Muḥammad is His servant and Messenger."

The Quran gives several prophets the honorable appellation of "servant":

> "The people of Noah denied before them; they denied Our **servant** and said, 'A madman,' and he was repelled.
> So he invoked his Lord, 'Indeed, I am overpowered, so help [me].'" (Quran 54:9-11)

> "[This is] a mention of the mercy of your Lord to His **servant** Zechariah." (Quran 19:2)

> "And to David We gave Solomon. An excellent **servant**, indeed he was one repeatedly turning back [to God]." (Quran 38:30)

> "Indeed, We found him (Job) patient, an excellent **servant**. Indeed, he was one repeatedly turning back [to God]." (Quran 38:44)

> "[Jesus] said, 'Indeed, I am the **servant** of God. He has given me the Scripture and made me a prophet." (Quran 19:30)

> "Exalted is He who took His **servant** (Muḥammad) by night from the Sacred Mosque to the Farthest Mosque, whose surroundings We have blessed, to show him of Our signs. Indeed, He is the Hearing, the Seeing." (Quran 17:1)

The Quran also relates the story of Moses and his young companion who went in search of a righteous servant (identified as Khidr) in possession of divinely-inspired wisdom.

> "Then they found a **servant** from among Our servants whom We had granted mercy from Us and whom We had taught knowledge from Us." (Quran 18:65)

It is significant to conclude this section by stating that Satan has no authority over the servants of God:

"Surely over My servants you have no authority. And sufficient is your Lord as a Wakīl (Guardian/ Disposer of affairs)." (Quran 17:65)

CONTINUOUS WORSHIP

When we recite the verse: "And I did not create the jinn and mankind except to worship Me", a question might arise: If worship is the purpose of my existence, how can I fulfill this purpose? How can worship be the ultimate aim of my existence while the combined total time of offering the five daily prayers may take up approximately an hour per day, or even less? A day is composed of 1,440 minutes; would I have fulfilled the purpose of my existence if I spent just 60 minutes in prayer per day?

This question may be answered when the essence of worship is clarified. Worship is not only devotional rituals such as prayer, recitation of the Quran, or supplication even though these are significant aspects of worship. When we consider narrations transmitted from the Infallible Imams which include the term "worship", we notice that worship encompasses many examples. Several ḥadīths mention forms of worship such as earning a lawful livelihood[1], gazing upon your parents with love[2], seeking knowledge, or thinking positively of God. In line with this, every favorable action that earns God's satisfaction is a form of worship. Therefore, every action you take has the potential of being transformed into an act of worship.

---

1. Biḥār al-Anwār. Volume 77, p.27.
2. Mīzān al-Ḥikma. Volume 20, p.1800.

Some people might mistakenly assume that prayer and religious rituals are the only forms of worship. It is transmitted that Jesus once asked a man: "What do you do?" The man answered: "I offer worship." Jesus then asked him who provided him with sustenance. When the man answered that it was his brother, Jesus answered: "Your brother is more worshipful than you."

When a person adheres to divine laws in obedience to God and in order to draw near to Him, s/he fulfills servitude in his/her individual and social life. When we recite: "You [alone] do we worship", this should be reflected in all aspects of our lives.

TRANSFORMATION OF ORDINARY ACTIONS INTO ACTS OF WORSHIP

You might ask yourself: How can I transform my everyday actions into worship? "Since worship is like nourishment for the spirit, the way oxygen is for the body, the more we infuse our day with acts of praise, the livelier our souls will feel. The question inevitably becomes: How can we be in a constant state of prayer when we have worldly obligations? The secret lies in the intention! Anything can be an act of worship if you make the intention of getting close to Allāh through that act."[1]

Our normal everyday actions may be transformed into acts of worship when they are accompanied by the intention of closeness to God. "An important aspect of any act of worship is the intention behind it. That is the

1. Secrets of Divine Love: A Spiritual Journey into the Heart of Islam.

factor that determines how a deed is judged – whether it is the fulfillment of an act of worship, a particular obligation, or any routine act. Through intentions, one's daily routine can be turned into worship or ibadah."[1] For instance, when you wake up in the morning and after performing fajr prayer, you can address God and say: "My Lord! Aid me so that I may perform all my actions today, whether inside my home or outside in society, sincerely for You."

In this manner, every minute of your life may be transformed into worship. "You must fill up your time with acts of worship so that no period of time elapses, whether by night or by day, without being used in some act of goodness. This is how the baraka within time is made manifest, the purpose of life fulfilled, and the approach to God the Exalted made constant."[2]

The effort to turn one's entire life and all one's thoughts, words, and actions into a pious endeavor which gains God's satisfaction is expressed in the following supplication mentioned in the Quran:

> "Say, 'Indeed, my prayer, my [ritual] sacrifice, my life and my death are for God, Lord of the Worlds.'" (Quran 6:162)

When you recite Sūrat al-Fātiḥa, make a firm decision to become a perpetual worshipper of God. "In Islam, worship consists of far more than the performance of ritual acts of worship, such as prayers and fasting. It

1. Islam, Muslims, and America, p.155.
2. Al-Haddad, Abd-Allāh. The Book of Assistance. Fons Vitae: 2003, p.17.

encompasses everything that one says, believes, or does for God's pleasure including: rituals, beliefs, social interactions, personal acts, community service, and other activities...The essence of ibadah is the feeling of gratitude towards God. In Islam, every action performed with the intention of pleasing God, or carrying out His commands, is considered to be an act of worship or ibadah. Acts that can be considered ibadah include visiting a sick person, helping a stranger, and forgiving someone."[1]

It is transmitted that a man once sought Imam Ja'far al-Ṣādiq (as) and remarked: "By God, we seek [the worldly life] and love to [gain] it." The Imam (as) asked: "What do you do with it?" He answered: "Through it, I benefit myself and my family, I maintain contact [with my relatives], I pay charity, and I go to Hajj and Umrah." The Imam (as) answered: "[This] is not a pursuit of the worldly life, but a pursuit of the hereafter."[2]

HOW SINCERE ARE WE WHEN WE RECITE "YOU [ALONE] DO WE WORSHIP"?

We recite this verse of Sūrat al-Fātiḥa numerous times per day during worship or for a devotional purpose, but what is the level of our sincerity? Do we truly ask assistance from God alone? When we recite "You [alone] do we worship", we should bear in mind that we must actively translate this verse into action, and embrace the life-transforming aspect of this verse.

1. Khan, Arshad. Islam, Muslims, and America. Algora Publishing: 2003, p.155.
2. Wasā'el al-Shī'a. Volume 12, p.19.

The path to sincere worship is not easy and various obstacles lie on the path such as the inclination of the human soul toward evil:

> "And I do not absolve myself [of blame], indeed the soul is prone to evil, except those upon whom my Lord has mercy. Indeed, my Lord is Forgiving [and] Merciful." (Quran 12:52)

Satan also lies in ambush and is intent on leading as many humans as possible astray:

> "[Satan] said, 'My Lord, because You have put me in error, I verily shall adorn the path of error for them in the earth, and I will mislead them all.
> Except, among them, Your chosen servants." (Quran 15:39-40)

> "[Satan] said, 'Because You have put me in error, I will surely sit in wait for them on Your straight path.
> Then I will come to them from before them and from behind them and on their right and on their left, and You will not find most of them grateful [to You]." (Quran 7:16-17)

In addition to instincts, morally corrupt social settings, and destructive media, there are numerous challenges which we face every day, and to maintain sincere worship we need God's aid. Through God's assistance we may overcome the soul's inclination to evil, frustrate Satan's ruses, and avoid corruption in society. Seeking God's aid is a form of tawakkol, reliance upon God. We should exert an effort and at the same time be fully aware that it is God, in His mercy and power, who grants us success in our efforts to draw near to him. The following supplication which is recited in the morning reflects this reality:

> "My God, if mercy from You does not begin with good success for me, then who can take me to You upon the evident path?
>
> If Your deliberateness should turn me over to the leader of hope and wishes, then who will annul my slips from the downfalls of caprice?
>
> If Your help should forsake me in the battle against the soul and Satan, then Your forsaking will have submitted me to where there is hardship and deprivation.
>
> My God, do You see that I have only come to You from the direction of hopes, or clung to the ends of Your cords when my sins have driven me from the house of union?"[1]

RESULTS OF SEEKING DIVINE ASSISTANCE

Requesting assistance from God bears favorable results, and in what follows are two important aspects:

a) Seeking divine aid facilitates advancement in the quest to obtain closeness to God. All material aspects of the worldly life are temporary and not worthy of competition. What truly deserves the exertion of effort

1. Dua Sabah (Morning Supplication), transmitted from Imam Ali (peace be upon him).

is the admittance to Heaven by purifying the soul and performing righteous deeds. Consider the following verses for example:

When God calls humans to fulfill worldly needs on Earth, notice the use of the word "walk" which denotes the advancement at a moderate/normal speed:

> "It is He who has made the earth subservient to you, so walk in its tracts and eat of His provision - and to Him is the resurrection." (Quran 67:15)

When God speaks of divine forgiveness and Heaven, the pace picks up and humans are urged to "hasten" toward repentance and their eternal abode:

> "And hasten to forgiveness from your Lord and a garden as wide as the heavens and earth, prepared for the God-fearing." (Quran 3:133)

In another instance, the word "race" is used:

> "Race with one another for forgiveness from your Lord and a Garden whose breadth is as the breadth of the heavens and the earth, prepared for those who believe in God and His messengers. Such is the bounty of God, which He bestows upon whom He wills, and God is of Infinite Bounty." (Quran 57:21)

And after speaking of a pure drink which the inhabitants of Heaven shall receive, the Quran states:

> "...So for this let the competitors compete." (Quran 83:25)

b) Through divine assistance, steadfastness is enforced and an individual is guarded from deviation. Hazards lie on the path, so you should always be cautious and never let down your guard. You should not be satisfied with any spiritual rank you reach or any good deeds you have performed. Even if a person spends a lifetime performing righteous deeds, there is always a danger of slipping on the path.

> "And do not take your oaths as [means of] deceit between you, lest a foot slip after it was [once] firm, and you would taste evil [in this world] for what [people] you diverted from the way of God, and you would have [in the Hereafter] a great punishment." (Quran 16:94)

We should always ask God for steadfastness on the path. The Quran relates how the believers faced the army of Goliath even though they were fewer in number. They recited the following supplication before the battle, and despite the odds achieved victory because they were sincere to their Lord:

> "And when they went forth to [face] Goliath and his soldiers, they said, 'Our Lord, pour upon us patience and plant firmly our feet and give us victory over the disbelieving people.'" (Quran 2:250)

DIVINE ASSISTANCE

It is important to note that requesting assistance from God differs from ordinary requests for aid from fellow humans. In circumstances when your mental and physical capacities are not sufficient to fulfill a task at hand, you seek help from someone who can aid you. You need to add someone's power to your own. But this is not the type of aid referred to in the holy verse. When you ask God to provide you with assistance, you don't independently rely on your capacities, skills or personal efforts. Whatever you are seeking, you should know that it is attainable only through God's aid. Everything you possess is merely a God-given blessing, and everything you accomplish occurs by the leave of God. It is important to know that the essence of assistance in the holy verse: "You [alone] do we worship and You [alone] do we ask for aid" is to know that God influences everything in this universe[1] and nothing has an impact without His permission.

1. Al-Yazdi, Misbah. Ilayka Ya Rab, pg.219.

Chapter Six:
Divine Guidance

اهْدِنَا الصِّرَاطَ الْمُسْتَقِيمَ ﴿٦﴾

6. Guide us to the Straight Path.

You can establish a sublime connection with God through Sūrat al-Fātiḥa. When you recite this holy sūra, you begin by mentioning God's attributes of mercy, and then move on to praise Him, mention His attributes of mercy once more, recognize His dominion over Resurrection Day, and then declare sincere worship and reliance upon Him. After that, you ask God to guide you to the Straight Path.

After the declarations of faith, what is worthy of request is asking God for steadfastness on the Straight Path. You are supplicating God, the Creator and Possessor of all things, the Lord of the Worlds. He has granted you the chance to call upon Him while millions of other human beings live in heedlessness. Your request should be in harmony with the purpose of your existence. Would it be suitable to ask God for wealth or social prominence and authority? While it is true that all favors are asked from God alone, yet the request of material possessions is not befitting when you are expressing the highest devotion to God. Material gains are limited and fleeting in nature. Life in this world is temporary, and it is inevitable that each and every one of us will be separated from that which s/he coveted in the worldly life. Could any rational person prefer temporary possessions over eternal divine favors and a life of everlasting bliss?

When a person is on the Straight Path, they ensure an eternality of favors. The following account points to the importance of asking God for a reward which is enduring and never perishes. A man named Rabi'a bin Ka'b served Prophet Muḥammad (s). It is transmitted that the Prophet (s) once asked him: "O Rabi'a, you have served me for seven years, won't you ask me something?" Rabi'a answered: "O Messenger of Allāh, give me time so I may think." On the morning of the next day, Rabi'a made an unexpected request: "[I want you] to ask Allāh, the Mighty and Majestic, to allow me to enter heaven with you." The Prophet (s) asked him: "Who taught you this?" Rabi'a answered: "O Messenger of Allāh, no one taught me, but I thought to myself and said: If you ask him (s) for money, it will be exhausted, and if you ask him (s) for a long life and children, their fate will be death." It is reported that Prophet Muḥammad (s) lowered his head a bit, and said: "I shall do so, but aid me with an abundance of prostration."

The significance of asking God to guide us to the Straight Path may be clarified through the following points:

1- God is the Light which pure hearts yearn for, and closeness to Him is the utmost source of tranquility.

> "O Man! You are laboring to your Lord laboriously, and you shall encounter Him." (Quran 84:6)

> "Indeed, to your Lord is the return." (Quran 96:8)

> "The path of Allāh, to whom belongs whatever is in the heavens and whatever is on the earth. Unquestionably, to Allāh do [all] matters come." (Quran 42:53)

A human's value lies in the attribution of his/her affairs to God, the source of all perfection.

> "Say, 'Indeed, my prayer, my rites of sacrifice, my living and my death are for Allāh, Lord of the worlds.'" (Quran 6:162)

2- Just as there is a Straight Path which leads to God, there are various ways which lead to perdition. The Holy Quran states:

> "And this is My path, which is straight, so follow it; and do not follow [other] ways, for you will be separated from His way. This has He instructed you that you may become righteous." (Quran 6:153)

Tyrants might make claims that they guide those under their yoke to a path of right conduct. For instance, the Holy Quran states the following:

> "Pharaoh said, 'I do not show you except what I see, and I do not guide you except to the path of rectitude.'" (Quran 40:29)

For this reason, we should always be careful which path we are following, and to avoid paths which are falsely presented as upright.

3- There are ways which lead to divine wrath "not of those who have evoked [Your] wrath" and others which are misguided "or of those who are astray", but a believer is cautious and asks God for guidance to the Straight Path.

> "By which Allāh guides those who pursue His pleasure to the ways of peace and brings them out from darkness into the light, by His permission, and guides them to a straight path." (Quran 5:16)

This path is distinguished by certain features:

1- It is close to the desired destination: There are certain ways which only serve in taking a person farther away from his/her intended destination with every step. "Those are called from a far place." (Quran 41:44) As for the Straight Path, it is a path which leads one swiftly to his/her destination. This concept may be clarified through the following example: The distance from one point to another while moving on a straight line is always shorter that the distance when following a crooked line. By following the Straight Path, an individual reaches ranks of closeness to God.

> "And when My servants ask you, [O Muḥammad], concerning Me - indeed I am near. I respond to the invocation of the supplicant when he calls upon Me. So let them respond to Me and believe in Me that they may be [rightly] guided." (Quran 2:186)

2- There is only one Straight Path, and it leads to spiritual ascent. On the other hand, there are several ways which take a person on a downward descent, moving him/her away from the ranks of closeness to God and pitching him/her into an abyss, to the "lowest of the low" (Quran 95:5).

> "And he upon whom My anger descends has certainly fallen." (Quran 20:81)

REFLECTIONS ON THE HOLY VERSE:

1- This verse, "Guide us to the Straight Path", forms a complete prayer which summarizes the most important thing which a person should ask for. Guidance is the greatest divine favor, and the Straight Path links the worldly life with the hereafter.

2- The request for guidance is in the plural form and not the singular. Guidance and salvation are not merely personal issues; the guidance and salvation of an individual are linked to those of the community. Social security is not only contingent on personal uprightness, but also on reform within the community.

> "And your Lord would not have destroyed the cities unjustly while their people were reformers." (Quran 11:117)

3- The Arabic word ṣirāt is translated as path. There are other Arabic synonyms which mean path/way such as ṭarīq and sabīl, so why is the term ṣirāt used in particular? In general, a ṭarīq may be smooth or bumpy, straight or crooked. As for the ṣirāt, it is a smooth path with no crookedness. According to some exegetes, the difference between ṣirāt and sabīl is similar to the above. Another explanation is that ṭarīq and sabīl may assume a material meaning in general usage, while a spiritual connotation applies to ṣirāt more than a material one.

4- There are narrations which indicate that there are two ṣirāts: The Straight Path of uprightness in the worldly life, and the Straight Path which shall lead the believers to heaven in the hereafter. The term ṣirāt may combine between the worldly life and the hereafter. The one who follows the Straight Path in the worldly life shall cross the ṣirāt of the hereafter, the bridge which every individual shall pass on Resurrection Day

DIVINE GUIDANCE

Al-Hadi, He who guides, is one of the Names of God. If God is the one who guides his creatures, where does human will fall? Why does God call people to guidance while it is in His hands? We may provide answers to these questions as follows:

1- **God is the Source of Guidance:** God is aware of every single movement in the universe, and every human action lies under God's ability and power.

> "And you do not will except that Allāh wills, the Lord of the worlds." (Quran 81:29)

> "And why did you, when you entered your garden, not say, 'What Allāh willed [has occurred]; there is no power except in Allāh'?" (Quran 18:39)

Guidance is attributed to God because if it were not for His will, no individual would have attained guidance.

> "And Allāh invites to the Home of Peace and guides whom He wills to a straight path." (Quran 10:25)

> "That is the guidance of Allāh by which He guides whomever He wills of His servants." (Quran 6:88)

2- **Divine Guidance is a Manifestation of the Wisdom of God.** The human intellect realizes that God in His wisdom would not leave His creatures without guiding them.

> "He said, 'Our Lord is He who gave each thing its form and then guided [it].'" (Quran 20:50)

God granted humans the freedom of choice and showed them the way, and He rewards or punishes them in the hereafter according to their deeds in the worldly life.

> "Are you recompensed except for what you used to do?" (Quran 27:90)

Guidance is a personal choice which means that God does not guide people by force. Some people may wonder: Why doesn't God forcibly guide all humans and lead them to the path of righteousness? The answer to this question may be clarified through a glimpse into the concept of perfection. A human is the khalīfa of God, and is responsible for self-rectification. Knowledge, patience, gratitude and benevolence are a few perfection traits, and so is free choice. Moral perfectibility which is attained through force has no value. If a human were forced to be righteous, there would be no difference between him/her and a robot which moves by the will of another.

Types of Guidance

1- **General Guidance:** There is a general form of guidance which God grants to every human on earth and is defined as "showing the way". God has guaranteed to show all humans the Straight Path and to lead them to its direction, but it is their personal decision to follow this path or not.

> "Indeed, We guided him to the way, be he grateful or be he ungrateful." (Quran 76:3)

This form of guidance is inclusive, and no one can argue that s/he has not received guidance, especially taking into consideration that God has taken it upon himself to guide humans.

> "Indeed, [incumbent] upon Us is guidance." (Quran 92:12)

This form of guidance occurs through several means:

A- **The Fitra:** There are instincts which are implanted in all human beings and values which do not change regardless of the passage of years or the region one lives in. For instance, everyone knows that it is necessary to express gratitude to someone who shows you kindness, a principle which the Holy Quran points to: "Is the reward for good [anything] but good?" (Quran 55:60) Additionally, every human instinctively realizes that oppression is wrong while acting justly is right. Suppose you visit a tribe living in the jungles of the Amazon rainforest or in the deserts of Africa, far away from all the tools of technology and separated from the outer world. Randomly choose one of its members and ask him/her: "Would it be morally correct to attack the house of a lone woman and her children and to seize their assets for personal gain?", the answer would certainly be: "No, that would be an act of transgression." This answer requires no previous human education or indoctrination; it is the reply of the universal fitra.

Belief in the Ultimate Source of perfection, power and knowledge who created the universe is an intrinsic belief, and so is the belief in life after death. These are forms of recognition present in all humans without any exception, even in atheists and tyrants who have concealed their fitra due to a variety of reasons.

B- **The Dispatch of Messengers:** The Holy Quran mentions that messengers have been sent to guide humans. Just as the fitra and the intellect are "inner messengers", the prophets are "outer messengers". Every human community throughout history has received guidance, and the Holy Quran clearly states that God sent a messenger to every nation:

"Indeed, We have sent you with the Truth, a bearer of glad tidings and a warner; and there is not a nation but a warner has passed among them." (Quran 35:24)

This warner may be a prophet, an infallible Imam, a spiritual scholar, or a righteous servant of God who confronts immorality and declares the Word of Truth. For instance, Sūrat Yāsin mentions the story of the three messengers and the righteous, unnamed man who rose to warn his people:

"And there came from the farthest end of the city a man, running. He said, 'O my people, follow the messengers.
Follow those who do not ask of you [any] payment, and they are [rightly] guided.
And why should I not worship He who created me and to whom you will be returned?
Should I take other than Him [false] deities [while], if the Most Merciful intends for me some adversity, their intercession will not avail me at all, nor can they save me?
Indeed, I would then be in manifest error.
Indeed, I have believed in your Lord, so listen to me.'" (Quran 36:20-25)

2- **Specific Guidance:** There is another form of guidance which is specific and marked by an active personal pursuit. When we recite numerous times per day during prayer "Guide us to the Straight Path", we are beseeching God to guide us to His Path. When you pray and recite Sūrat al-Fātiḥa, you are declaring that you have already seen the path and recognized it. What form of guidance are we then asking for? It is to "reach the destination." You have discovered the Straight Path through your mind and heart, but you need God's providence in order to remain steadfast on this path, to display true servitude, attain perfection, and reach eternal bliss.

Suppose you are lost in a foreign city and ask a passerby for directions. If s/he only gives you verbal directions, s/he would have merely provided you with information (this may be compared to general guidance). But if another passerby offers to personally accompany you to your destination, then this form of guidance may serve to clarify our example. Not only does God provide His sincere and devoted servants with general guidance, He also bestows a specific form of guidance upon them.

> "So those who believe in Allāh and hold fast to Him - He will admit them to mercy from Himself and bounty and guide them to Himself on a straight path." (Quran 4:175)

> "And those who are killed in the cause of Allāh - never will He waste their deeds.
> He will guide them and improve their state,
> And admit them to Paradise, which He has made known to them." (Quran 47: 4-6)

REQUIREMENTS OF GUIDANCE

In His wisdom, God ordained that matters should occur according to the law of causation. If the causes are fulfilled, then results will come into effect. For instance, God is Al-Razzāk, the one who grants sustenance. He is able to profusely bestow favors upon humans without them exerting the slightest effort, but He does not want His creatures to remain idle. Hence, the human pursuit of sustenance is in itself a reason to gain sustenance. How could a person who lazily sits behind a locked door and asks God for favors expect to receive them?

Similarly, guidance is in the hands of God, but it is important to remember that He has created a rule for guidance with requirements and conditions. We may name this rule the "law of guidance". For instance, a matchstick includes the chemical components which enable combustion; it catches fire when it is struck and with the presence of suitable conditions such as the absence of water or humidity. Likewise, the law of guidance stipulates that an individual should fulfill certain conditions and overcome specific obstacles in order to attain guidance.

1- **Conditions of Practical Guidance:** There are conditions which God has placed and which humans should actively and voluntarily pursue in order to gain guidance. Faith and the performance of righteous deeds may be considered the most important of these conditions.

> "Indeed, those who have believed and done righteous deeds - their Lord will guide them because of their faith. Beneath them rivers will flow in the Gardens of Pleasure." (Quran 10:9)

It is noticeable that the aforementioned verse mentions that God will guide these individuals "because of their faith". Due to their voluntary adoption of faith, God grants them a special form of mercy. Another verse emphasizes the importance of faith and "holding fast" to God in order to receive guidance:

> "So those who believe in Allāh and hold fast to Him - He will admit them to mercy from Himself and bounty and guide them to Himself on a straight path." (Quran 4:175)

Additionally, purifying oneself–described as a jihad, a struggle- is a means to receive divine guidance. Those who strive for God, purifying their souls, strengthening their willpower, and preserving themselves from moral deviation, will gain guidance. Purification of the self is a voluntary human action –done through assistance from God- and what follows is a divine bestowal: guidance.

> "And those who strive for Us - We will surely guide them to Our ways. And indeed, Allāh is with the doers of good." (Quran 29:69)

Furthermore, taqwa is a critical factor to receive guidance. Taqwa is the observance of all religious duties and the avoidance of sins. For instance, even though the Holy Quran presents knowledge for all mankind to benefit from, yet practical divine guidance is restricted to the mutaqin.

> "This is the Book whereof there is no doubt, a guidance for the mutaqin (the God-fearing)." (Quran 2:2)

2- **Obstacles to Divine Guidance:** As previously mentioned, guidance is intricately linked to human choice. When a person consciously chooses falsehood and immorality over the Truth and morality, s/he would have barred divine guidance. The Holy Quran mentions several obstacles which obstruct divine guidance.

- Disbelief (Kufr):

> "Indeed, Allāh does not guide the disbelieving people." (Quran 5:67)

- Wrongdoing (Thulm):

  "Indeed, Allāh does not guide the wrongdoing people." (Quran 5:51)

- Disobedience (Fisq):

  "And Allāh does not guide the [defiantly] disobedient people." (Quran 9:24)

- Conscious Selection of Misguidance:

  "[Even] if you should strive for their guidance, [O Muḥammad], indeed, Allāh does not guide those He sends astray, and they will have no helpers." (Quran 16:37)

- Dishonesty:

  "Indeed, Allāh does not guide he who is a liar [and] an ingrate" (Quran 39:3); "Indeed, Allāh does not guide one who is a transgressor [and] a liar." (Quran 40:28)

Therefore, the Holy Quran clarifies that disbelief, performance of evil deeds, dishonesty, disobedience to God, and consciously choosing misguidance over guidance are all obstacles to divine guidance. We may compare God's guidance to the sun which sends its comforting rays over the earth; some people choose to remain hidden from it while others embrace its light and warmth. God is always ready to grant us His love, care and assistance, to remove us from darkness and lead us to the light, but He also expects us to ask for His guidance "until the vision of our hearts pierces the curtains of light to reach the core of supremacy, and that our souls become suspended by the majesty of Your Holiness."[1]

Sometimes, we might notice individuals who do not refrain from sinning, and when admonished they say: "I will stop when God guides me" or "I am waiting for His guidance." This is a weak excuse. On Judgement Day, no one can claim that God did not bestow guidance upon him/her. God has clarified the path of guidance, and the person who stubbornly and defiantly chooses not to follow that path has only himself to blame.

There is a historical tale of a man named Al-Fuḍayl ibn □Iyāḍ, who was a chief of a gang that launched raids against caravans in the desert and robbed them of their possessions. The bandits would bring Fuḍayl what they had stolen and he would proceed to distribute the spoils among them. Despite his crimes, Fuḍayl diligently offered his five daily prayers. It is recounted that he was on a raiding expedition one day with a number of thieves. After robbing the caravan and sitting down to rest, one of the members of the pillaged caravan ventured to ask a thief after the identity of the chief of bandits.

> "He is praying in a tent."
>
> "But it is not time for prayer!" The poor man protested.
>
> "He is offering supererogatory prayers."
>
> "Why is he not eating with you?"
>
> "He is fasting."
>
> "But it is not the month of Ramadan!"

---

1. Munajat Sha'baniyah.

"He is offering a supererogatory fast."

The man was astounded and headed toward Fuḍayl whom he found praying to defiantly object: "You steal and pray?!"

Fuḍayl answered: "Have you read the verse: 'And [there are] others who have acknowledged their sins. They had mixed a righteous deed with another that was bad. Perhaps Allāh will turn to them in forgiveness. Indeed, Allāh is Forgiving [and] Merciful.'"

The man's confusion increased and he did not know what to say, and Fuḍayl was not deterred.

Fuḍayl was known not to raid the caravans of poor people nor to seize the possessions of women. One story of his banditry relates how a rich merchant, fearful of running into bandits, mistook Fuḍayl for an honest man and asked him to hide the majority of his wealth lest bandits find him. As the merchant continued on his way, he was robbed of his remaining wealth by Fuḍayl's men. When the merchant returned to Fuḍayl to recover the majority of his wealth, he was dismayed to find the bandits who had robbed him surrounding the man he had trusted. However, Fuḍayl expressed that he was a god-fearing man, and would not betray his trust, therefore motioning the merchant to reclaim the wealth he had left in trust with him despite the protestations of the bandits.

However, one day was to prove fateful in the life of Fuḍayl. He spotted an approaching caravan and decided to monitor its movements at midnight in order to formulate a plan for the upcoming robbery. When Fuḍayl drew near to the caravan, he heard a man's voice reciting the following Quranic verse from a tent: "Has the time not come for those who have believed that their hearts should become humbled at the remembrance of Allāh and what has come down of the truth?" (57:16) Upon hearing this holy verse, Fuḍayl was shaken to the core and decided to repent. He had been aware that he was deviating from God's commands by pillaging other people's possessions, but he had resisted repenting and turning back to the path of guidance. But in a crucial moment, a holy Quranic verse awakened him, and he decided to mend his deeds and return sincerely to God. Through his repentance, Fuḍayl became a living example of the following Quranic verses:

> "So is one whose breast Allāh has expanded to Islam and he is upon a light from his Lord [like one whose heart rejects it]? Then woe to those whose hearts are hardened against the remembrance of Allāh. Those are in manifest error.
> Allāh has sent down the best statement: a consistent Book wherein is reiteration. The skins of those who fear their Lord shiver from it, then their skins and their hearts soften to the remembrance of Allāh. That is the guidance of Allāh by which He guides whom He wills. And one whom Allāh leaves astray - for him there is no guide." (Quran 39:22-23)

It is worth noting that God describes one who enjoys this guidance as being "upon a light from his Lord". When a person's heart expands to Islam, a light penetrates it. Darkness dissipates and the Straight Path lies ahead, wide and clear.

SPECIFICATION OF THE STRAIGHT PATH

Linguistically, the word ṣirāt means the "easy path", while mustaqīm means "straight, that which suffers no crookedness". If a person desires to attain closeness to God, there is only one path –the Straight Path. Exegetes have differed in their opinions regarding the definition of the Straight Path and have offered a range of options such as Islam, Quran, monotheism, servitude to God, the fitra, or the path of the prophets. These suggestions may all be combined in one; the Straight Path begins with embracing God's religion and believing in the messages of the prophets, and involves adhering to God's revelation and performing all religious duties. It is the path of uprightness which links a servant with God.

> "Say: Indeed, my Lord has guided me to a straight path - a correct religion - the way of Abraham, inclining toward truth. And he was not among those who associated others with Allāh." (Quran 6:161)

It is transmitted that Imam Ja'far al-Ṣādiq (as) explained the meaning of the Straight Path as follows: "Guide us to persist on the path which leads to your love, conducts to your paradise, and prevents [us] from following our whims and expiring, or following our opinions and perishing."

This path has been trodden by the prophets and righteous individuals throughout history. The prophets gave tidings of prophets who came after them, and the greatest tidings were those of our most beloved Prophet Muḥammad (s) upon whom was revealed the Quran, the divine Book to be followed until the Day of Judgment.

Hence, the Straight Path is the path of Prophet Muḥammad (s) and his Household.

> "Ya Sin,
> By the wise Qur'an.
> Indeed you, [O Muḥammad], are one of the messengers,
> On a straight path." (Quran 36:1-4)

> "And indeed, you call them to a straight path." (Quran 23:73)

> "And thus We have revealed to you an inspiration of Our command. You did not know what the Book was nor [what the] faith was, but We have made it a light by which We guide whom We will of Our servants. And indeed, [O Muḥammad], you guide to a straight path,
> The path of Allāh, to whom belongs whatever is in the heavens and whatever is on the earth. Unquestionably, to Allāh do [all] matters return." (Quran 42: 52-53)

The Straight Path is distinguished by the following features:

1- It is only a single path, while following other ways would lead to misguidance:

> "And this is My path, which is straight, so follow it; and do not follow [other] ways, for you will be separated from His way." (Quran 6:153)

2- It is the path of uprightness, and those who follow it are steadfast:

> "Allāh keeps firm those who believe, with the firm word, in the worldly life and in the Hereafter. And Allāh sends astray the wrongdoers. And Allāh does what He wills." (Quran 14:27)

3- It is the path which allows an individual to come close to God.

> "And when My servants ask you, [O Muḥammad], concerning Me - indeed I am near. I respond to the invocation of the supplicant when he calls upon Me. So let them respond to Me and believe in Me that they may go aright." (Quran 2:186)

4- It is the path of security, and one who follows this path suffers no loss, sadness or fear:

> "Those who believe and do not mix their belief with injustice - those will have security, and they are [rightly] guided." (Quran 6:82)

Overcoming Obstacles to Guidance

God wants His servants to proceed on the Straight Path, with strong determination and firm steps. It is critical to start with a solid resolution, and this in turn becomes stronger when one overcomes difficulties and obstacles. Any worldly feat requires perseverance, and -with all the more reason- so does the most sublime human endeavor: the spiritual journey to God. Yet there are certain obstacles which hinder progress and these need to be overcome:

Satan

We can summarize Satan's ultimate goal as follows: leading humans astray. From the moment you wake up in the morning until you place your head on your pillow at night before falling asleep, Satan is working to cause you to stumble and sin. Satan insolently mentioned this aim after his eviction from divine mercy, as the Holy Quran states:

> "[Satan] said, 'Because You have put me in error, I will surely sit in wait for them on Your straight path.
> Then I will come to them from before them and from behind them and on their right and on their left, and You will not find most of them grateful [to You].'" (Quran 7:16-17)

Even though "I will surely sit in wait for them on Your straight path" are Satan's words and a rule followed by his soldiers among the jinn, yet this declaration may be considered the mode of conduct followed by the representatives of Satan. These may be immoral human individuals and even corrupt media and unethical publications. The method followed by such representatives is to target those who follow the Straight Path, and attack them from four directions:

"Before them": This may indicate future events such as upcoming temptations and desires or fears of poverty as Satan tries to convince humans that they will become impoverished if they pay charity.

"Behind them": This may indicate the offspring one leaves behind. For instance, Satan might tempt a human to gain wealth and status, even through unlawful means, to ensure a life of riches for his/her descendants.

"On their right and on their left": Al-yamin, which means the "right side" in English, is an Arabic word which also denotes noble matters since they are performed with the right hand. In this holy verse, the reference to this word might denote how Satan strives to misguide humans in matters regarding religion. As for the "left side", it may be a reference to Satan's adornment of immorality in order to lure humans to falsehood.

Personal Desires

When a person receives guidance from God, s/he has acquired a grand divine favor which leads to salvation in the hereafter.

> "Say, Indeed, the guidance of Allāh is the [true] guidance." (Quran 2:120)

But on the path of guidance, one must always be cautious. Perhaps the worst idol is personal desire:

> "Have you seen he who has taken as his god his [own] desire, and Allāh has sent him astray out of knowledge and has set a seal upon his hearing and his heart and put over his vision a veil? So who will guide him after Allāh? Then will you not be reminded?" (Quran 45:23)

Al-hawa is the inclination of the soul toward what it desires. This tendency is naturally present in humans, and when applied correctly serves in fulfilling religiously approved matters such as the multiplication of progeny and the construction of the earth. But this inclination might deviate from the right course and gradually lead humans to "the lowest of the low". Therefore, moderation is required as it marks the Straight Path. It is incorrect to prevent the self from the divinely-approved matters it seeks, and likewise it is unacceptable to indiscriminately and completely surrender to personal desires. It is important to strike a balance and avoid the two following errors:

1) **Neglect of personal needs:** Could it be possible that the wise God who created humans and granted them basic physical needs would not allow them to appease these natural instincts? No religious teachings can be considered valid if they do not take the needs of human beings into account. Religion does not involve physical suffering or the eradication of natural urges. In fact, neglecting the body's needs may result in psychological problems and functional defects.

   It is recounted that a companion of Prophet Muḥammad (s), Othman bin Math'oun, was diligent in worship. He even asked the Prophet (s) if it was religiously recommended to isolate in the mountains for worship. Othman bin Math'oun fasted by day and spent his nights in prayer, and even refrained from sexual relations with his wife who sought Prophet Muḥammad (s) to file a complaint regarding her husband. After hearing her, it is transmitted that Prophet (s) summoned Othman and said: "O Othman! Allāh the Exalted did not send me with monasticism, but He has sent me with the easy, lenient ḥanīfiyya. I fast, I pray, and I touch my wife. He who loves my fitra should follow my Sunnah..."

2) **Falling into excess:** The human self, if left unchecked, is characterized by a tendency to go beyond what is sufficient. When the self comes into possession of a certain thing, it asks for more and is not satisfied with what satiates its needs. The pursuit of worldly possessions, when done through divinely-approved means, is not a cause for criticism, but one must always remain cautious so that material gains are not transformed into an aim in themselves. The insatiable greed for riches might reach a level where a person is ready to sacrifice the hereafter for the sake of the worldly life.

> "Those are the ones who have bought the life of this world [in exchange] for the Hereafter, so the punishment will not be lightened for them, nor will they be aided." (Quran 2:86)

Therefore, it is important to keep a close watch on the soul and place restrictions on its desires.

The Holy Quran mentions an unnamed individual, which exegetes identify as Balaam son of Beor, who followed his own personal desire and detached himself from the signs of God,

> "And recite to them the news of him to whom we gave Our signs, but he detached himself from them; so Satan pursued him, and he became of the deviators.

> And if We had willed, we could have elevated him thereby, but he adhered [instead] to the earth and followed his own desire." (Quran 7:175-176)

It is said that Balaam son of Beor was a scholar among the Israelites during the time of Moses. It is recounted that, due to Balaam's faith and knowledge, Moses relied on him in matters relating to calling people to God. However, when Pharaoh strove to sow division between those who aided Moses in his confrontation, he enticed Balaam with material temptations. Balaam proved to be weak in heart and gradually deviated from the Truth and followed his desires. In the end, Balaam completely detached himself from faith until he lost the spiritual ranks he had gained. This illustrates that when desire takes hold of a human being, he becomes a slave to his ego and personal interest, and his opinions, logic, emotions and stances begin to revolve around personal desire.

It is recounted that a king once said to an ascetic: "Why do you not come to my castle even though you are my slave." The ascetic answered: "O king, if you only knew, you would have discovered that you are the slave of my slave, for I control my desire but desire controls you."

Many positions we take may seem rational but are in fact shrouded by personal desire. For instance, if one possesses wealth, his "mind" might deem it unacceptable to allot a sum of the savings s/he has earned "with personal intelligence and effort" to poor people; if one is a staunch follower of a political party, s/he might blindly accept all this party's proclamations; if one belongs to a certain racial group, s/he might fanatically justify injustices committed by its members. Seldom do two individuals disagree among themselves and one is willing to admit that s/he is wrong. We love ourselves so much, and one is blind to the faults of his beloved! This is all due to the fact that personal desire has shackled and blinded the intellect, until we begin to believe that personal desires are rationally justified.

The greatest challenge we face is to confront our personal desire. Sūrat al-Najm describes Prophet Muḥammad (s) in the following two verses:

> "Nor does he speak from [his own] desire.
> It is not but a revelation revealed." (Quran 53:3-4)

Since Prophet Muḥammad (s) never followed his personal inclination, he was upon a Straight Path. Therefore, in order to be guided to the Straight Path, we must fully adhere to the following Quranic verses:

> "But as for he who feared the position of his Lord and prevented the soul from [unlawful] desire,
> Then indeed, Paradise will be [his] refuge." (Quran 79: 40-41)

Other Means of Deviation

There are numerous means of deviation from the Straight Path mentioned in the Holy Quran. Evil emanates not only from Satan. Every individual, group or nation which acts according to the following declaration "I will surely sit in wait for them on Your straight path" becomes a form of devil.

> "And thus We have made for every prophet an enemy - devils from mankind and jinn, inspiring to

one another decorative speech in delusion." (Quran 6:112)

Not only should a person keep away from all forms of misguidance, s/he must also refrain from causing others to be led astray, whether deliberately or unknowingly.[1]

---

1. It is recounted that an oppressive monarch decided to impose the consumption of swine-meat on his people for economic purposes. He decided to make the consumption of pork a general habit by forcing his people to consume the flesh of swine under the threat of death. To enforce his decision, he decided to invite a venerable clergyman to eat swine meat in his presence and in front of the public. This invitation deeply grieved the clergyman who prayed to God for guidance. The chief of guards, an admirer of this clergyman, decided to find a solution which would preserve his life so he devised a plan which he secretly related to the clergyman. He would clandestinely agree with the cooks of the castle to place mutton on the clergyman's plate instead, and the clergyman would proceed to eat this religiously-approved meat while the rest of the attendants would eat swine meat. Thus, he would consume lawful meat and at the same time preserve his life. But at the banquet and in the presence of the attendees, a thought crossed in the mind of the clergyman after the meat was placed before him: I know that this meat is lawful to consume, but what shall I do regarding all these people? They are unaware that I am consuming lawful meat, and if they see me eating then it would become easier for them to consume swine meat and I would then bear the burden of their imitation of my actions on Resurrection Day. When the monarch ordered him to eat, the clergyman refused to the fury of the king and was thrown in the most notorious of jails, awaiting execution. In confinement, the chief of guards went to see him and emphasized that the meat he had served him was religiously lawful and that he would never betray him, but the clergyman answered that what prevented him from eating was the fear of

CONTRIBUTORS TO GUIDANCE

Just as there are means of deviation which cause people to go astray, there are also certain conditions which contribute to the guidance of humans to the Straight Path. Some will be mentioned as follows:

I'tisam

I'tisam in this context denotes holding fast to God in the face of temptations which drive people away from the Truth. Holding fast to God involves seeking His power alone and placing trust only in His disposal of affairs. 'Isma means immunity and invincibility which prevents an individual from transgressing divine law. For instance, the Holy Quran uses a derivative of this term when referring to Prophet Joseph's restraint, where his unsuccessful seductress states: "That is the one on whose account you blamed me. And I certainly sought to seduce him, but he **ista'sam**" (Quran 12:32) which is translated as firmly refused, abstained, or proved continent.

I'tisam is a mental state where a person constantly senses the omnipotent presence of God, and this serves to prevent the individual from following personal desire and disobeying God. Any individual can develop control over his impulses and actions and exercise restraint not only in the face of sins but even in the face of thinking of sinning. There are believers who would never even think of committing an immorality, drinking alcohol or stealing

---

leading people astray as they looked upon him as a source of guidance. In the end, the clergyman was executed.

other people's property. Thus, one must strengthen this 'isma and allow it to permeate all aspects of life.

> "And whoever holds firmly to Allāh has [indeed] been guided to a straight path." (Quran 3:101)

As there are matters which naturally strengthen the body's immunity against viruses, 'isma resembles a spiritual immunity. But in order to acquire 'isma and hold firmly to God, a person should first reject Satan and all his representatives, and express belief in God and declare allegiance to His prophets.

> "So whoever disbelieves in Ṭāghūṭ and believes in Allāh has grasped the most trustworthy handhold with no break in it. And Allāh is Hearing [and] Knowing." (Quran 2:256)

Furthermore, one must constantly place his thoughts and actions under surveillance and voluntarily refrain from committing sins as they injure one's 'isma. This may be illustrated in a phrase from Du'a Kumayl, the famous supplication transmitted from Imam Ali (as): "O Allāh, forgive me those sins which tear apart safeguards!"

Submission and Obedience to God and His prophets

God would never in His wisdom forsake guiding mankind to moral perfectibility and the means to eternal bliss. "Indeed, [incumbent] upon Us is guidance" (Quran 92:12). Thus, when a person consciously chooses to follow guidance, God's compassion and care will encompass him and lead him to the straight path.

> "And so those who were given knowledge may know that it is the truth from your Lord and [therefore] believe in it, and their hearts [humbly] submit to it. And indeed is Allāh the Guide of those who have believed to a straight path." (Quran 22:54)

This holy verse signifies two important aspects: One is intellectual, as faith is acquired by an intellectual process, while the other is psychological-behavioral as demonstrated in the humble submission to God. When you conclude by logic that God is the wise lord who knows what is best for His creatures, you will submit all your affairs to Him. We seek specialists for advice, doctors for medical prescriptions, engineers for construction projects and lawyers for legal counsel. Therefore, by priority we should rely on the Lord of the Worlds who has created us, is acquainted with all of our affairs, and knows what is best for us.

It is related that in the time of Prophet Muḥammad (s), there was a man named 'Awn bin Malek whose son had been taken captive and who had fallen into poverty and hardship. 'Awn decided to see the Prophet (s), seeking relief. Prophet Muḥammad (s) counseled him to be patient and to submit his affairs to God: "Fear Allāh, be patient, and often repeat: There is no might or power except with Allāh." 'Awn carried out the Prophet's (s) advice and submitted his affairs to God. It was not long before his living conditions changed to the better and his son was able to escape form captivity and return safely to his father.

The greatest joy is steadfastness on the Straight Path. God sent infallible prophets to guide people to this path, and submission to Him entails submission to His prophets. For instance, Satan's sin was not his refusal to prostrate to God, but his arrogance which drove him to refuse to bow down to Adam as God had ordered.

> "He said, 'I am better than him. You created me from fire and created him from clay.'" (Quran 38:76)

Similarly, one of the reasons that certain nations rejected faith is their refusal to follow the prophets God had sent them, despite the logical proof and miracles pointing to the truthfulness of these prophets. For example, God sent Moses with nine clear signs but Pharaoh arrogantly refused to express faith in Moses' message.

> "And Pharaoh called out among his people; he said, 'O my people, does not the kingdom of Egypt belong to me, and these rivers flow beneath me; then do you not see?
> Or am I [not] better than this one who is insignificant and can hardly make [his meaning] clear?'" (Quran 43:51-52)

For this reason, submission to Prophet Muḥammad's (s) orders is a criterion and test of faith:

> "But no, by your Lord, they will not [truly] believe until they make you, [O Muḥammad], judge concerning that over which they dispute among themselves and then find within themselves no discomfort from what you have judged and submit in [full, willing] submission." (Quran 4:65)

Imam Ja'far al-Ṣādiq (as) and Imam Mūsa al-Kāthem (as) had a pious companion named Safwan who hired his camels for pay. One day, Safwan visited Imam Imam Mūsa al-Kāthem (as) who said to him: "O Safwan, everything in you is meritorious except one thing."

"May I be sacrificed for you, what action is that?" asked the perplexed Safwan.

"You hire your camels to Harun al-Rashid."

Safwan then clarified that he did not hire his camels for hunting or games but for offering the pilgrimage to Mecca, and that he did not serve Harun himself, but ordered his slaves to accompany the caliph on the journey."

The Imam (as) asked: "Do they pay you in advance or after their return?"

"After they return", he replied.

"Do you not carry the hope that they return safe and sound from their journey so that you receive your payment?"

"Yes."

The Imam (as) said: "One who wishes for them to remain alive is [connected to] them, and one who [is connected to] them will go to Hell."

These words had an impact on Safwan who then sold all his camels. When Harun heard of this he summoned him and asked him about the reason. Safwan answered that he had become old and weak and was unable to take care of the camels anymore, and that even his slaves are not capable of maintaining them properly. Harun was not convinced, but nonetheless, Safwan realized that the Straight Path required a heart which does not wish for the endurance of oppressors.

Sometimes, humans might encounter religious rulings which come against their interests and desires, and they might attempt to avoid these rulings to preserve their own personal gains. They do this despite the fact that God's commands and prohibitions are for their own good. Adherence to God's laws, as stated by Prophet Muḥammad (s), is a necessary prerequisite and a practical commitment to the verse "Guide us to the Straight Path".

> "And whatever the Messenger has given you – take it; and [from] what he has forbidden you –refrain [from it]." (Quran 59:7)

> "Say, 'Obey Allāh and obey the Messenger; but if you turn away - then upon him is only that [duty] with which he has been charged, and upon you is that with which you have been charged. And if you obey him, you will be [rightly] guided. And there is not upon the Messenger except the [responsibility for] clear notification.'" (Quran 24:54)

Attachment to the Holy Quran

The content of the Holy Quran –the doctrines, ethical values, logical arguments, laws, stories of the prophets, parables, and more- is a content which enables humans to follow the Straight Path.

> "This is the Book whereof there is no doubt, a guidance for the God-fearing." (Quran 2:2)

> "O mankind, there has to come to you instruction from your Lord and healing for what is in the breasts and guidance and mercy for the believers." (Quran 10:57)

> "This [Quran] is enlightenment for mankind and a guidance and a mercy for a people who are certain [in faith]." (Quran 45:20)

> "...There has come to you from Allāh a light and a clear Book.
> By which Allāh guides those who pursue His pleasure to the ways of peace and brings them out from darknesses into the light, by His permission, and guides them to a straight path." (Quran 5:15-16)

In what follows, we will mention two important points which enforce attachment to the Holy Quran:

A- Recitation of the Holy Quran and Contemplation of its Verses:

God, the Light of the Heavens and the Earth, has revealed a Light –the Holy Quran- which guides humans. It is the Word of God, and every individual should strive to form a bond with the Quran marked by affection, reverence, recitation and adherence to all of its commands.

> "So believe in Allāh and His Messenger and the Light which We have sent down. And Allāh is Well-Acquainted with what you do." (Quran 64:8)

It is important not to confine the Holy Quran to mere ceremonial proceedings such as sending the reward of recitation to a deceased person, or limiting recitation to certain occasions such as funerals. The Quran is a book of life, "a guidance for the God-fearing", and this entails that every individual should strive to attain an in-depth reading of the Holy Quran and to remove all veils which prevent the light of the Quran from permeating into the heart.

> "So when you recite the Quran, seek refuge in Allāh from Satan the outcast." (Quran 16:98)

There are spiritual fruits which one reaps from the Holy Quran. For instance, the following holy verse gives tidings to the believers that the Quran grants them steadfastness and guidance.

> "Say, [O Muḥammad], 'The Holy Spirit has brought it down from your Lord in truth to make firm those who believe and as guidance and good tidings to the Muslims.'" (Quran 16:102)

Consistent recitation of the Quran, with an accurate understanding of its meanings, awakens the heart and soul. This influences a person, even on the long term, as opposed to those who forsake the Quran entirely and whose hearts have become hardened. Recitation reaches a higher degree when it is combined with contemplation.

> "Then do they not reflect upon the Qur'an, or are there locks upon [their] hearts?" (Quran 47:24)

Acting in Conformity with the Holy Quran

When you recite a verse, ask yourself: What is the message that God wants to deliver? How do my actions compare with respect to this verse? After recitation and contemplation of the verses of the Holy Quran, it is essential to translate faith into action.

> "...But if they had done what they were instructed, it would have been better for them and [a] firmer [position for them in faith].

> And then We would have given them from Us a great reward.
> And We would have guided them to a straight path." (Quran 4:66-68)

Prophet Muḥammad (s) was a living manifestation of the verses of the Holy Quran. When asked about the ethics of the Prophet (s), one of his wives answered: "His ethics was the Quran." The Quran leads to the Straight Path, and thus inevitably Prophet Muḥammad (s) is on the Straight Path: "Indeed you, [O Muḥammad], are one of the messengers, On a straight path", and he guides to the Straight Path: "And indeed, [O Muḥammad], you guide to a straight path."

Therefore, acting in accordance with the Holy Quran is the means to proceed on the Straight Path. In this manner, the Quran becomes the beacon for individual and social conduct and a means for worldly comfort and eternal bliss.

> "And if only they upheld [the law of] the Torah, the Gospel, and what has been revealed to them from their Lord, they would have consumed [provision] from above them and from beneath their feet." (Quran 5:66)

Thus, "upholding" the Quran means applying all individual and social laws according to the Quran. This will come to effect at a worldwide level in the future, when the pious shall inherit the earth:

> "And verily we have written in the Scripture, after the Reminder that My righteous servants will inherit the earth." (Quran 21:105)

GUIDANCE TO THE STRAIGHT PATH

As previously mentioned, guidance occurs by adhering to the Quran which illuminates the way to God, and following the example of Prophet Muḥammad (s). There are several narrations transmitted from the Imams regarding the meaning of the holy verse: "Guide us to the Straight Path". For instance, it is transmitted that Imam Ali (as) explained it as follows: "Perpetuate the success with which we have obeyed you in our past days, so that we can obey you in the future of our lives."[1] Additionally, a narration transmitted from Imam Ja'far al-Ṣādiq (as) states: "It means guide us to persist on the path which leads to your love, conducts to your paradise, and prevents [us] from following our whims and expiring or taking our opinions and perishing."

We may summarize guidance to the Straight Path according to Quranic verses and ḥadīths as follows:

1- **To follow the way of moderation,** avoiding extremes or excesses in all life aspects.

> "And those who, when they spend, are neither extravagant nor niggardly, but are ever, between that, [justly] moderate." (Quran 25:67)

2- **To constantly persevere in the purification of the soul.** This does not imply negligence of the body's needs. An individual can purify his soul while at the same time satisfying his physical needs in a religiously lawful manner and avoiding transgressions. Through

1. Al-Kashani, Mohammad. Al-Safi. Volume 1, p.85.

self-rectification, one continues to progress in attaining closeness to God.

> "And those who strive for Us - We will surely guide them to Our ways. And indeed, Allāh is with the doers of good." (Quran 29:69)

3- **To continuously monitor your heart.** Avoid spiritual emptiness and eradicate any moral illnesses such as arrogance, greed, envy and malice from your heart.

> "And do not disgrace me on the Day they will be raised,
> The Day when there will not benefit [anyone] wealth or children,
> But only one who comes to Allāh with a sound heart." (Quran 26:87-89)

4- **To obey the commands of God and Prophet Muḥammad** (s). Reason leads us to conclude the necessity of obeying God, and it is God who has ordered us to obey His Prophet.

> "And whatever the Messenger has given you – take it; and [from] what he has forbidden you – refrain [from it]." (Quran 59:7)

> "And indeed, you call them to a straight path." (Quran 23:73)

5- **To maintain a sincere intention.** The Straight Path is the direct and nearest way between God and his servant, and to proceed on this path once must have sincerity.

> "And they were not commanded except to worship God, [being] sincere to Him in religion, ḥunafā'

(inclining to truth), and to establish prayer and to give zakah; and that is the right religion." (Quran 98:5)

6- **To strengthen willpower.** Determination is necessary so that one does not retreat or falter on the Straight Path when faced with challenges and difficulties.

"So be patient, [O Muḥammad], as were those of determination among the messengers..." (Quran 46:35)

7- **To acquire knowledge from its original source.** This ensures uprightness and prevents from falling into deviation. Thus, one identifies the Straight Path through reasoning and expresses gratitude for the favor of his Lord.

"And Allāh has revealed to you the Book and wisdom and has taught you that which you did not know. And ever has the favor of Allāh upon you been great." (Quran 4:113)

Finally, in order to be guided to the Straight Path, one must rise and strive actively and energetically to fulfill this aim. God did not create humans merely to satisfy their physical needs. What difference would there be between humans and animals then? Man is the khalīfa, the vicegerent, of God, and it is appropriate for this vicegerent to voluntarily pursue perfection. This requires constant awareness, which may be aided through the daily recitation of Sūrat al-Fātiḥa.

Ask God to guide you to the Straight Path, and keep in mind that this initially requires the fulfillment of certain conditions, which may be exemplified by the following passage from Du'a Kumayl: "My Lord! Strengthen my limbs in Your service and fortify my ribs in determination. Bestow upon me earnestness in my fear of You, and continuity in my being joined to Your service so that I may move easily toward You in the fields of the foremost, and hurry to You among the prominent, and desire fervently Your proximity among the fervently desirous, and draw near to You with the nearness of the sincere, and fear You with the fear of those who have certitude."

We always need God's help as the daily Morning Supplication states: "If Your help should forsake me in the battle with the soul and Satan, then Thy forsaking will have entrusted me to where there is hardship and deprivation."

Chapter Seven:

Heavenly Favor

صِرَاطَ الَّذِينَ أَنعَمتَ عَلَيهِمْ غَيرِ المَغضُوبِ
عَلَيهِمْ وَلاَ الضَّالِّينَ ﴿٧﴾

7. The path of those upon whom You have bestowed favor,

not of those who have evoked [Your] wrath or of those who are astray.

After pleading God to guide us to the path of uprightness, Sūrat al-Fātiḥa clarifies that that there are three paths which humans take. Only one of them leads to God's satisfaction. The first path is that of those who have earned God's favor; the second path is that of those who have evoked God's wrath, while the third path is that of those who have gone astray and have no hope of reaching the desired end.

Through your own will you may pursue the path of guidance or the path of misguidance, and consequently the path you voluntarily take will determine your eternal fate. God, the All-Wise, has created humans with freedom of choice. Through this choice one achieves transcendence or plummets into moral degradation. Every person has been entrusted with a grand responsibility as the final outcome of his/her choices in life is either eternal bliss or permanent perdition. Sūrat al-Fātiḥa teaches us that we should we ask God to guide us to the Straight Path and it also informs us that there are two other paths, and this emphasizes the necessity of asking God for that one required path.

REFLECTIONS ON THE HOLY VERSE:

1- God describes the people of the Straight Path as those upon whom He has bestowed His favor. Would that mean that those who have incurred His wrath or those who have gone astray are not recipients of His favors in the worldly life?

We can answer this question as follows. God does not hold back His favors in the worldly life from humans in general. Many irreligious people enjoy favors from God whether in wealth or general well-being. There is no correlation between religiosity and the reception of worldly favors. With this in mind, it is important to remember that a favor is in reality a favor when it is employed for righteous action, but if it is not fittingly made use of it turns into a curse. This is akin to a person who uses his wealth and beauty for immoral purposes.

"They recognize the favor of Allāh; then they deny it. And most of them are disbelievers." (Quran 16:83)

In the aforementioned holy verse, there is a possibility that the word "favor" mentioned therein is the favor of being guided to the Straight Path which the disbelievers have rejected.

2- Mention of those upon whom God has bestowed favor points to two important things which may be deduced from the other two descriptions. These individuals are not astray, which means that they are rightly guided; and they have not incurred God's wrath which means that God is pleased with them. This grants them a special status.

> "Allāh being pleased with them, and they with Him. That is the great triumph." (Quran 5:119)

3- "Those upon whom You have bestowed favor" is mentioned in the past tense which may indicate that the Straight Path is one which many righteous individuals have chosen to take throughout history, in different times, places and circumstances. We are not the only ones who are following this path. Many have passed before us on earth who have struggled, toiled, and persisted to gain God's grace –probably in more difficult conditions than ourselves- and have striven toward moral perfection and ultimately God's pleasure.

> "A multitude of those of old, And a multitude of those of later time." (Quran 56: 39-40)

The following report is narrated on the authority of Khabbab bin Al-Arat: "We complained to Allāh's Messenger (s) (of the persecution inflicted on us by the infidels) while he was sitting in the shade of the Ka'ba, leaning over his Burd (covering sheet). We said to him, 'Would you seek help for us? Would you pray to Allāh for us?' He said, 'Among the nations before you, a (believing) man would be put in a ditch that was dug for him, and a saw would be put over his head and he would be cut into two pieces; yet that (torture) would not make him give up his religion. His body would be combed with iron combs that would remove his flesh from the bones and nerves, yet that would not make him abandon his religion. By Allāh, this religion (Islam) will prevail till a traveler from Sana (in Yemen) to Hadrarmaut will fear none but Allāh, or a wolf as regards his sheep, but you (people) are hasty.'"

4- Evoking God's wrath is an effect of committing corrupt actions, while going astray is a cause which leads to farness from God and true bliss. As for the Quranic phrase "those upon whom You have bestowed favor", we may state that it combines both cause and effect. Displaying high ethics and performing righteous deeds is a means to gain divine favor. Furthermore, the ensuing result -which is the attainment of God's pleasure and passage to heaven- is also a divine favor.

5- The Quranic phrase "those upon whom You have bestowed favor" attributes great value to guidance to the Straight Path. There are many forms of divine favors which are too numerous to count, as the holy Quran states:

> "And He gave you from all you asked of Him. And if you count the favors of Allāh, you cannot enumerate them. Indeed, man is unjust [and] ungrateful." (Quran 14:34)

Nevertheless, the highest favor is guidance to the path which leads to eternal bliss. Material favors are limited and short-lived, but the blessing of guidance has long-term effects.

6- The phrase "those upon whom You have bestowed favor" includes the subject "You", but the phrase "those who have evoked [Your] wrath or of those who are astray" does not mention God as the subject. This may be an indication that misguidance is a result of the corrupt actions of humans themselves.

> "The different qualities of the paths followed by the three categories mentioned in this verse are revealed by the different ways in which they are presented. Those whom Thou hast blessed conveys an action performed by God in the past tense, thus giving a sense of finality and certitude in that God's blessings and favor upon them have already occurred."[1]

THE PEOPLE OF FAVOR

In the Holy Quran, God mentions different divine favors to remind humans of Himself, the source of every grace. This constant remembrance of God's favors contributes to one's own perfection because it results in gratitude to God. God awakens us to the fact that blessings are not only material in nature (these are limited in time and space), but that there are favors much greater than those which are seen by the naked eye. Spiritual gifts are

1. The Study Quran, p.61.

of superior quality and lead in turn to everlasting and unlimited favors.

Your presence in this life is a divine favor. The opposite of existence is non-existence; therefore, all other favors are attached to this favor. How would you gain any blessing if you didn't exist in the first place?

As previously mentioned, there are two types of blessings: material and spiritual. God mentions various favors in the Holy Quran; in Sūrat al-Naḥl alone there are 13 verses which mention the favors God has granted to mankind.

- Sustenance:

  "...and [He] has provided for you from the good things. Then in falsehood do they believe and in the favor of Allāh they disbelieve?" (Quran 16:72)

- Domestic Quarters:

  "And Allāh has made for you from your homes a place of rest and made for you from the hides of cattle tents which you find light on your day of travel and your day of encampment; and from their wool, fur and hair is furnishing and enjoyment for a time." (Quran 16:80)

- Shelter and Garments:

  "And Allāh has made for you, from that which He has created, shadows and has made for you from the mountains, shelters and has made for you garments which protect you from the heat and garments which protect you from your [enemy in] battle. Thus does

> He complete His favor upon you that you might submit [to Him]." (Quran 16:81)

This sūra additionally states:

> "And if you would count the favors of Allāh, you could not enumerate them. Indeed, Allāh is Forgiving [and] Merciful." (Quran 16:18)

FORMS OF SPIRITUAL FAVORS

There is a variety of spiritual favors which God bestows upon mankind, with guidance to the Straight Path being one of the most significant. In what follows is a list of spiritual favors granted by God to humans:

1- **Dispatch of Prophets:** The role which God entrusted to His prophets is to deliver humans from darkness into light. The presence of divinely-guided figures is a major blessing as they call people to God and deliver His message:

> "And (remember) when Moses said to his people: O my people! Remember Allāh's favor unto you, when He placed among you prophets, and made you kings, and gave you that (which) He gave not to any (other) of (His) creatures." (Quran 5:20)

2- **Revelation:** Not only did God send prophets to guide mankind, but He also sent a form of guidance which would remain after the death of the prophet. Being human, every prophet lived for an appointed lifespan so it was necessary for a more permanent form of favor which would serve to guide humans to the Straight

Path after the death of the prophet, and that is: divine books.

> "And remember the favor of Allāh upon you and what has been revealed to you of the Book and wisdom by which He instructs you." (Quran 2:231)

3- **Religion:** It is a form of divine grace to adhere to God's religion; to follow a set of fundamental beliefs and ethical guidelines, and to adhere to a body of law which dictates every action. This divine grace aids humans in pursuing their perfection, especially when it is coupled with the appointment of Imams who lead the way. The following verse, revealed on the day of Ghadir Khom, displays this reality:

> "This day I have perfected for you your religion and completed My favor upon you and have approved for you Islam as religion." (Quran 5:3)

4- **Obedience to God:** Have you ever stopped and considered that the acts of obedience you offer to God are in themselves a form of divine favor? When you obey God and refrain from sinning, you revel in one of the greatest favors which God grants to His servants, a favor with an eternal significance. When you obey God, divine favors envelop you from all sides: you have followed God's Prophet (s), you have soundly made use of your logic which has led you to the Truth, and your heart has accepted God's message.

It is transmitted that Prophet Muḥammad (s) had a servant named Thawban who loved the Prophet (s) immensely and longed for his presence when he was away. One day, it was noticed that Thawban's face changed in color and his body became thin. When the Prophet (s) saw him in such a condition, he asked him about himself and Thawban answered: "O Messenger of Allāh! I am not ill nor have I any pain. When I do not see you, I long for you until I rejoin you. Then I remember the hereafter and fear that I will not be able to see you there, for I have discovered that you will be raised [in a high station] with the prophets; if I enter paradise, I will be in a position lower than yours and if I do not enter paradise then I would never be able to see you."

It is transmitted that the Prophet (s) answered Thawban: "By the One in whose Hand is my soul, no servant [of God] believes until I am more beloved to him than his soul, his parents, his wife, his children and all people." It is reported that due to Thawban's inquiries, the following holy verse was revealed[1]:

> "And whoever obeys Allāh and the Messenger - those will be with the ones upon whom Allāh has bestowed favor of the prophets, the steadfast affirmers of truth, the martyrs and the righteous. And excellent are those as companions." (Quran 4:69)

The following supplication also indicates that obedience to God is a favor granted by Him: "O Allāh, grant us the success of obedience and remoteness from disobedience..."[2] It is also a divine favor when one is inspired to the remembrance of God, as the following supplication transmitted from Imam 'Alī al-Sajjād

1. Al-Tabarsi, Muḥammad. Mujamma' Al-Bayan, Volume 3-4, 110.
2. Al-Kaf'ami, Ibrahim. Al-Misbah. Supplication of Imam Mahdi.

indicates: "Among your greatest favors upon us is the flow of Your remembrance on our tongues and Your permission for us to supplicate You, declare You exalted, and glorify You!"[1]

Remembrance is the return of the ignorant person to the All-Knowing One, the poor person to the Self-Sufficient One, and the weak individual to the Capable One, and this is a divine grace.

5- **The Convening of Hearts:** Brotherhood in faith is a distinguishing feature and a consequence of belief, displayed by those who have purified their hearts from moral illnesses such as envy, spite, arrogance, and the love of hegemony. Without the expulsion of negative attributes, believers would not be able to live peacefully, cooperatively, or lovingly among themselves.

No philosophical or educational system can guarantee a life of brotherhood and mutual harmony among humans in the worldly life. The reason is that the main condition for the establishment of such brotherly ties is the purification of the self and immunity in the face of temptations, and this is only facilitated by God.

> "And remember the favor of Allāh upon you - when you were enemies and He brought your hearts together so you became, by His favor, brothers." (Quran 3:103)

> "And brought together their hearts. If you had spent all that is in the earth, you could not have brought their hearts together; but Allāh brought

1. Al-Sahifa Al-Sajjadiyya, Munajat al-Thakirin.

them together. Indeed, He is Mighty [and] Wise." (Quran 8:63)

The Holy Quran mentions that life in paradise involves the removal of any rancor from the hearts of the believers.

"And We will remove whatever is in their breasts of resentment, [so they will be] brothers, on couches facing each other." (Quran 15:47)

6- **Divine Protection:** God protects and guards the believers as the Holy Quran states: "Allāh is the Guardian of those who believe." (Quran 2:257) The favor of divine protection is manifest during moments of hardship and challenges

"O' you who have believed, remember the favor of Allāh upon you when a people were determined to extend their hands [in aggression] against you, but He withheld their hands from you; and fear Allāh. And upon Allāh let the believers rely." (Quran 5:11)

Exegetes of the Holy Quran mention that this verse was revealed during the sixth year of the hijra, after the pagans, under the command of Khalid bin Walid, decided to ambush the Muslims while they were preoccupied with offering the noon prayer. Prophet Muḥammad (s) discovered the conspiracy and offered the noon prayer in the format of the prayer of fear (which is composed of two rak'ahs and involves a group which prays and another which stands guard over the ones offering prayer), therefore frustrating the pagans' plans. This verse is a general rule which comes into effect at all times.

7- **Reward of Righteous Deeds in the Hereafter:** God bestows His favors upon us in the hereafter as well, in the form of the divine reward granted for righteous actions in the worldly life. This divine reward is the most sublime form of divine favor because it is eternal and unperishable. God is so benevolent that the effort we exert in the performance of righteous deeds is a favor, and the reward granted for these deeds is a divine favor as well.

> "They rejoice in a favor from Allāh and bounty, and that Allāh does not waste the reward of the believers." (Quran 3:171)

THOSE WHO HAVE EVOKED GOD'S WRATH

God created humans and breathed into them of His spirit so that they may receive His mercy and be guided to the Straight Path. He distinguished them among His creatures and provided them with the means to pursue His satisfaction and forgiveness. God treats us with the utmost compassion, to the extent that –according to the Holy Quran- the reward for one good deed is ten good deeds, and good deeds erase bad deeds. Then what causes God's wrath upon humans?

The anger of God is not hasty, nor does it descend in vain. This means that the person who incurs God's wrath has greatly transgressed, reaching extreme levels of ingratitude, arrogance, and violation of God's commandments. There are verses in the Holy Quran which mention some characteristics or actions which anger God:

1- **At the Ideological Level:** Despite the manifest signs of God's greatness and grace, those who have incurred God's wrath live in doubt, lead lives of hypocrisy, and think negatively of God:

> "And [that] He may punish the hypocrite men and hypocrite women, and the polytheist men and polytheist women - those who assume about Allāh an assumption of evil nature. Upon them is the evil turn [of fortune]; and Allāh has become angry with them and has cursed them and prepared for them Hell, and evil it is as a destination." (Quran 48:6)

2- **At the Psychological Level:** Those who have chosen disbelief over belief expel all light from their hearts. Additionally, their disbelief increases with the passage of time.

> "But he who opens [his] breast to disbelief, upon them is wrath from Allāh, and for them is a great punishment." (Quran 16:106)

3- **At the Behavioral Level:** A corrupt intellectual and psychological background is reflected in conduct. For instance, the Holy Quran mentions how God bestowed His grace upon the Children of Israel. Not only did God save them from the tyranny of Pharaoh: "O Children of Israel, remember My favor which I have bestowed upon you and that I preferred you over the worlds" (Quran 2:47), He provided them with sustenance during their wandering in the desert "And We shaded you with clouds and sent down to you manna and quails" (Quran 2:57); provided them with water "And We inspired Moses when his people implored him for water, 'Strike with your staff the stone,' and there gushed forth from it twelve springs" (Quran 7:160); and sent numerous prophets to guide them. Despite all of these divine favors, the Israelites transgressed.

> "They have been put under humiliation [by Allāh] wherever they are overtaken, except for a covenant from Allāh and a rope from the people. And they have drawn upon themselves anger from Allāh and have been put under destitution. That is because they disbelieved in the verses of Allāh and killed the prophets without right. That is because they disobeyed and [habitually] transgressed." (Quran 3:112)

Some of the Children of Israel distorted the words of God: "Of the Jews there are those who change words from their context" (Quran 4:46); became involved in usury and the illegitimate consumption of wealth: "And their taking of usury while they had been forbidden from it, and their consuming of the people's wealth unjustly" (Quran 4:161); refused to fight with Moses and Aaron "They said, 'O Moses, indeed we will not enter it, ever, as long as they are within it; so go, you and your Lord, and fight. Indeed, we will sit here"; and transgressed to the extent of killing God's prophets: "And for their breaking of the covenant and their disbelief in the signs of Allāh and their killing of the prophets without right and their saying, 'Our hearts are wrapped'. Rather, Allāh has sealed them because of their disbelief, so they believe not, except for a few" (Quran 4:155).

It is important to point out that any nation -regardless of its religion- which acts similarly to the Children of Israel will face the same fate and incur God's wrath. Disbelief, transgression, distortion of God's words, and the denial of Truth will lead to divine anger.

> "And he upon whom My anger descends has certainly fallen." (Quran 20:81)

THOSE WHO ARE ASTRAY

The term ḍalalah (misguidance) and its derivatives are mentioned 191 times in the Holy Quran. In addition to misguidance or the state of being astray, this term may denote waste and ineffectiveness as in the following verse: "Those who disbelieve and avert [people] from the way of Allāh - He will **waste** their deeds" (Quran 47:1). At other times it describes forms of misconduct such as manifest or extreme misguidance:

> "Then woe to those whose hearts are hardened against the remembrance of Allāh. Those are in manifest misguidance." (Quran 39:22)

> "The ones who prefer the worldly life over the Hereafter and avert [people] from the way of Allāh, desiring to make it (seem) deviant. Those are in extreme misguidance." (Quran 14:3)

"Addressing the psychology of being astray, 28:50 asks rhetorically, Who is more astray than one who follows his caprice without guidance from God?"[1] Misguidance is the antithesis of guidance and is composed of various degrees: Some misguided people are unheedful of their misguidance, other are hesitantly astray, while some others are full deniers. The description of misguidance is applied in the Quran to those who have transferred their belief into disbelief, to the pagans, the disbelievers, the sinners, those who insult God and His Prophet (s), those who deny the Truth, and even the Muslims who take the disbelievers as allies.

In Sūrat al-Fātiḥa, we may reach the following conclusions regarding "those who are astray":

1- "Those who are astray" may be spiritually and behaviorally less corrupt than those who have incurred God's wrath.

2- "Those who are astray" are lost but may not necessarily insist on leading others astray.

3- "Those who are astray" might reach a level of misguidance where they incur God's wrath. When one goes astray from the path of guidance and refuses to return to the Truth when s/he receives warning, then s/he starts to join those who have incurred God's wrath.

4- All of those who have incurred God's wrath are astray, while not all of those who are astray have incurred God's wrath.

5- There are certain narrations which describe the Christians as "those who are astray" and the Jews as those who have evoked God's wrath. Regardless of the

1. The Study Quran, p.61.

authenticity of these narrations or lack thereof, this remains a significant example because the person who does not know the Truth is not to be equated with one who knows the Truth but deliberately rejects and distorts it.

Postscript

A LESSON FROM AN AFFLICTED MAN

It is said that Jesus Christ was once passing through the desert. He found a man lying on the ground like a corpse, unable to see nor rise up. The only sign of life was the movement of his lips. Jesus drew near to him and heard him say: "Praise be to God who has exempted me from what He has tested others."

Jesus wondered about the meaning of these words. What test was the man exempted from, even though he was afflicted with disease and could hardly move a limb? The man explained: "He has exempted me in that He has placed faith in my heart [enabling me] to thank Him for all that has befallen me."

God had granted the man firm belief, contentment and patience, but many other humans are deprived of these favors. One who is deprived of faith suffers from true misfortune, even if s/he does not sense it!

Jesus was deeply affected by the man's answer and asked him if there was a need, he could fulfill for him.

The man answered, "Yes. My son cares for me by providing me with food and drink. He has not come for three days, and I do not know what has befallen him."

Jesus went in search of the man's son and discovered that he had been attacked by wolves in the desert and met his death. He traced his steps to the man and compassionately informed him of the sad news. The man raised his head to the sky and said: "Praise be to God who has not left a lament in my heart for this world. I had clung to the world out of love for my child. My Lord, if you will..."

And his soul ascended to God.

A BEDOUIN ON THE VERGE OF DEATH

Someone said to a Bedouin in his final moments: "You are going to die."

The Bedouin asked "Where shall I be taken?"

The answer came: "To God."

The Bedouin replied: "I do no hate to go to the One from whom I have only seen good."

A LESSON FROM AN IMPOVERISHED MAN

A man went to a clergyman to complain of his poverty and the lack of divine favors he was receiving. The clergyman asked him: "Would you be pleased if you were blind but you possessed ten thousand dirhams?"

The man answered: "No"

"Would you be pleased if you were mute but you possessed ten thousand dirhams?"

"No," he replied again.

> "Would you be pleased if your arms were severed but you possessed ten thousand dirhams?"

The same answer once more came: "No"

The clergyman then counselled him: "You complain of the lack of God's favors while you are immersed in His favors! Beware from ingratitude because it turns blessings into curses."

***

It is true that some people enjoy abundance while others suffer from privation, but a contented heart knows that any divine bestowal is a blessing which one can never express full gratitude for. A greedy person, however, looks upon abundance as a deficiency and is not satisfied with what s/he has been given.

There are numerous means to attain satisfaction, driving the heart toward gratitude. One way is to look at those who lack divine favors while you bask in them. On the other hand, when an individual looks at the temporary worldly grants which have been given to others, they might underestimate the blessings which they already enjoy.

www.ingramcontent.com/pod-product-compliance
Lightning Source LLC
Chambersburg PA
CBHW051559010526
44118CB00023B/2753
* 9 7 8 0 9 9 5 7 5 8 9 5 7 *